COUTURE CHOCOLATE

WILLIAM CURLEY

Photography by Jose Lasheras

jacqui
small

For Suzue, my inspiration, and our
adorable daughter, Amy Rose.

First published in 2011 by **Jacqui Small** Llp

an imprint of Aurum Press Ltd,

The Old Brewery, 6 Blundell Street

London N7 9BH

United Kingdom

www.Quartoknows.com

Publisher Jacqui Small

Editors Abi Waters & Emma Callery
Managing Editor Kerenza Swift
Designer Robin Rout
Photography Jose Lasheras
Production Peter Colley

British Library Cataloguing-in-Publication Data
A catalogue record for this book
is available from the British Library.

ISBN 978-1-906417-59-8

10 9 8

Printed and bound in China

Notes on measurements:
All recipes contain metric and imperial measurements
followed by US/Australian cup conversions for relevant
ingredients. Use one set of measurements only and
not a mixture. US/Australian terms have also been
included in brackets where relevant.

CONTENTS

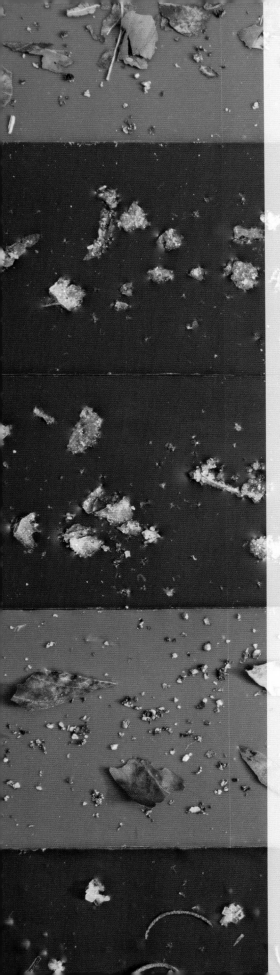
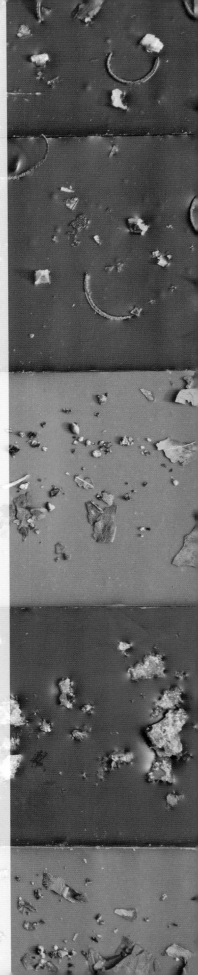

FOREWORD

I was very pleased that William approached me to write this foreword for his eagerly anticipated book. In my 35 years in the business very few artists have come along as good as William – he is a fantastic pastry chef and outstanding chocolatier.

He was an enthusiastic young lad when he started working for me at La Tante Claire – always giving 100%, asking questions, trying out new recipes and methods, continually striving to create innovative and exciting dishes by constantly pushing the boundaries and challenging his ability.

The foundation in my kitchen was making everything from scratch, not very common in restaurant kitchens at that time. I believe that chefs should be able to have the freedom to make what they want, do what they want and become the chef that they aspire to be. This is a philosophy that William shares and has followed throughout his career. As a chef you are constantly learning, every minute of every day, you can never know it all, there is no finish line.

William entered my kitchen at La Tante Claire as a commis chef, responsible for petit fours, and left as an extremely talented pastry chef. He continued to grow his career by building his foundations and gained ground by working at some of the world's most renowned restaurants. Later William became Chef Patissier at *The Savoy*, where he met his wife Suzue. William and Suzue now have two incredible chocolate and patisserie shops in Richmond and Belgravia. In Paris there are a vast number of fine patisseries and chocolate shops, but in the UK there are very few and if you are going to visit one, William Curley's should definitely be at the top of your list.

This book is a detailed insight into William's chocolates and patisseries and the ideas and inspirations behind his innovative flavour combinations and should have pride of place in every chocolate lover's kitchen.

Pierre Koffmann

AN APPROACH TO CHOCOLATE

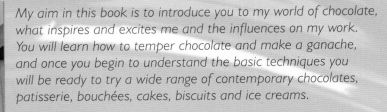

My aim in this book is to introduce you to my world of chocolate, what inspires and excites me and the influences on my work. You will learn how to temper chocolate and make a ganache, and once you begin to understand the basic techniques you will be ready to try a wide range of contemporary chocolates, patisserie, bouchées, cakes, biscuits and ice creams.

I grew up on the East coast of Scotland and although my grandmother was a wonderful cook I could never have dreamt that I would one day carve out a career as a patissier-chocolatier. I left school with no formal qualifications and enrolled at a local college and was immediately drawn to cooking – bakewell tart, chocolate éclairs and Dundee cake… it was hard to resist. Two years later I became an eager apprentice at Gleneagles Hotel in Perthshire under the legendary Ian Ironside and my love affair with being a patissier-chocolatier had begun. My career was now in full flow and the kitchen of Pierre Koffmann's three-Michelin-starred restaurant, La Tante Claire, beckoned. He really opened the door for me and sent my career in the right direction; from there the great chefs Raymond Blanc, Marco Pierre White, Anton Edelmann and Marc Meneau have all instilled the most important aspect of my work… never compromise.

I have always believed in using the very best ingredients – the finest couverture is essential, everything should be fresh and natural, avoiding artificial preservatives, flavourings and additives. It is important for young chefs to have a strong foundation in their work. For me, as you will see in this book, taking classical dishes and recipes and modernizing is very important. You'll find classic patisserie such as Mille-feuille (see page 166) through to Japanese-inspired Apricot & Wasabi Chocolates (see page 72). I also want to make people smile with the Orange Teacakes (see page 126) and Chocolate Coconut Bar (see page 114) – our homage to famous chocolate bars. I enjoy being creative and experimenting with new dishes and combinations – looking for marriages that you wouldn't imagine is also a great challenge.

Through Suzue I am very much inspired by Japan, with it's vibrant patisserie and chocolate scene, but I always cherish my trips to France – it wasn't so long ago, before Eurostar, that I would jump on the night bus to Paris and spend the weekend wandering the streets, gazing into the patisserie and chocolate shops and eating their wares, dreaming that one day I would have my own shop.

I am very enthusiastic about training and developing young people. Our business is full of apprentices, many of whom are now running the various sections within our kitchen. In our craft it is so important to teach and inspire the next generation.

CHOCOLATE ESSENTIALS

THE DISCOVERY OF COCOA

Wild cacao was originally consumed as long ago as 1500BC by the Olmecs. It is thought that they were the first humans to make it into a drink by crushing cocoa beans and cooking them with water and spices, such as chillies.

The Olmecs were the first to develop successful methods of cultivating, followed over time by the Aztecs and the Mayans. Soon, the cocoa bean became a powerful commodity in Meso-America, used as a monetary unit and as part of religious rituals.

In 1502 Christopher Columbus was given a bag of cocoa beans when he landed on the Island of Guanaja, but he did not appreciate its potential value. Then, in 1519, Hernán Cortés arrived on the coast of present-day Mexico and embarked on his famous conquest of the Aztec empire. The true importance of this brown gold was not recognized until Cortés drank it with the Aztec emperor Montezuma, and the invading Spanish then used local produce (such as sugar cane, vanilla, cinnamon and pepper) to adapt it to their tastes. On his return home, Cortés was in disgrace for not finding real gold and so it was not until 1544 that chocolate was officially brought to Spain by a visiting party of Mayan dignitaries.

During the 17th century, cocoa began arriving at other ports throughout Europe, effortlessly conquering every region's palate. In the latter part of the century, chocolate and coffee shops, such as The Coffee Mill and Tobacco Roll (some of the first gentleman's clubs) started opening up all over London and in 1674 they started offering chocolate in the form of pastilles, and then later in baked goods like cakes.

Dutchman, Coenraad J. Van Houten, invented the world's first hydraulic chocolate press for separating cocoa butter (the pale yellow, edible vegetable fat extracted from the cocoa bean) from the cocoa mass, thus extracting and separating two-thirds of the fat. The remaining cake was considered more digestible and so, for the first time, cocoa powder was manufactured. He also patented the addition of an alkali to cocoa powder (creating dutched cocoa) giving it a darker and more red colour, combatting it's natural acidity and therefore improving it's flavour.

In 1847, building on Van Houtens inventions, J. S. Fry & Sons of Bristol developed chocolate as we know it today for the first time. They created a way of adding cocoa butter back into the dutched chocolate, adding sugar and thus creating a paste that could be moulded. The result was the first chocolate bar.

With the Industrial Revolution in full swing, chocolate companies opened all over Europe and the chocolate industry had begun.

Opposite: Amedei (see page 16) cocoa pods, cocoa beans and cocoa nibs from the Caribbean.

Origins of Cocoa

Cocoa originates from South America, growing in Venezuela, Ecuador, Mexico and the Caribbean. These native countries continue to grow cocoa today and are noted for producing some of the best cocoa in the world.

The cocoa tree lives in the lower canopy of the rainforest with mother trees protecting their fragility from excessive wind or rain. Cocoa grows best in high humidity 10–20° latitude either side of the equator, which is how cocoa migrated across the globe. The plants flourish in a very humid atmosphere at about 20–35°C (68–95°F) along the west coast of Africa, Madagascar, Indonesia and also Malaysia.

There are three varieties of the cocoa tree:

Criollo The Criollo pod produces a small amount of cocoa beans of superior quality, delicate in flavour yet also complex. The Criollo only represents 2–3% of the world's cocoa market and is native to Central America, but is now also grown in the Caribbean.

Forastero The Forastero is the most common cocoa pod and now makes up 85% of the world population. This is due to its hardy nature and ability to produce large yields. Although native to the Amazon it makes up all of Africa's cocoa crops.

Trinitario The Trinitario is a hybrid of the Criollo and the Forastero cocoa varieties. It originates from Trinidad after an introduction of Forastero to the local Criollo crop.

Cocoa pods are cut from the trees by hand with machetes or long-handled tools.

Cocoa beans are carefully removed from the pods once they have been cut open.

Cocoa nibs are what remain once the husks and shells of the cocoa beans are removed.

Cocoa mass is the name for the paste that is produced when the nibs are crushed.

Cocoa butter is removed from the cocoa mass by being pressed or drained.

Cocoa powder is the residue left behind when the cocoa butter has been removed.

Couverture chocolate is the final stage of chocolate making, which is achieved when cocoa butter is added to cocoa mass and then processed with sugar and vanilla.

Theobroma cacao (cocoa tree) originated in South America but has migrated across the world as far as Western Africa, the Caribbean and Malaysia. There are 5–6 million cocoa farmers worldwide, and 40–50 million people depend on cocoa for their livelihood.

The cocoa tree produces two harvests a year, one larger crop and a secondary crop. Harvest periods depend on the country of growth. Ripe cocoa pods are harvested by cutting the pod from the tree or knocking it off with a stick. The pod is then sliced in half and the beans and the surrounding pulp are scooped out. They are then placed into large wooden crates, usually lined with banana leaves – the sweet pulp aids the fermentation process that develops the flavour of the cocoa. The fermentation takes around 4–6 days.

The beans are then spread out onto large trays and allowed to dry naturally in the sun; sun drying also adds flavour to the cocoa – it generally takes around 1–2 weeks. The dried beans are then graded and packed into hessian sacks and shipped to a chocolate manufacturer. When the beans arrive they are lightly roasted to develop the flavour. The beans are then put through a machine where they are crushed, husks are removed and the cocoa nibs are graded.

The nibs are ground by passing through a series of rollers to make the cocoa mass or liquor. The cocoa mass, together with extra cocoa butter, sugar and vanilla (and potentially soya lecithin) are placed in a mixer that pulverizes and kneads together the chocolate, which at this stage will be gritty on your palate. To make it taste completely smooth and silky, the mixture now has to be conched (which will also take away any remaining bitterness). 'Conch' comes from the Spanish word *concha*, which means shell, and the original vessel used to hold the chocolate was shaped like a conch shell. At Amedei, granite rollers grind the chocolate to a velvety texture. The characteristic taste, smell and texture of chocolate are developed at this stage. It takes up to 12 hours for commercial chocolate; however, for premium chocolate it takes much longer (about 40–70 hours).

Opposite: Blocks of couverture chocolate.

CHOCOLATE IN PRACTICE

Choose your ingredients with care and be prepared to shop around until you find what you are after. Whatever you choose to make, never compromise on your ingredients.

Chocolate Breakdown

Couverture Chocolate This is the best-quality chocolate, which we always recommend using for our recipes. It contains 32–39% cocoa butter, which means that the chocolate, together with correct tempering, will have a crisp snap when broken, a rounded flavour and a lovely sheen. The high amount of cocoa butter used in makes it easier to work with, providing a finer coating shell than chocolate that contains a smaller percentage of cocoa butter. When a bar of chocolate lists a percentage of cocoa solids, this is the cocoa mass and cocoa butter, the remainder is made up of sugar, vanilla and sometimes soya lecithin.

Couverture chocolate is the most important ingredient in our business and in our opinion the brand Amedei really does lead the way. All of our recipes, in our shops and this book, are developed to work the best characteristics of Amedei's chocolate.

Based in the small town of Pontedera in Tuscany, Amedei produce fine chocolate from only the Trinitario and Criollo beans and produce the most rounded and complex blends that we use for all our creations. They source some of the world's finest beans, and every stage of the process is dealt with the utmost care. Amedei give over 70 hours of conching to each blend, ensuring they produce a very unique chocolate. There is no soya lecithin in their chocolate, which can result in the chocolate being slightly thicker, particularly when tempering, so do beware.

There are a handful of other fine chocolate producers such as Valrhona, Michel Cluizel, Pralus and Amano. I have included in the Directory *(see page 224)* where to buy quality couverture chocolate and my advice would be to shop around and taste a lot until you find the couverture chocolate that you enjoy.

Dark chocolate gives a richness and intensity to any chocolate recipe. We mostly use dark chocolate in our products as the natural flavours are much more prominent. We would recommend using a dark chocolate with at least 60% cocoa solids. US dark chocolate is referred to as 'bittersweet', – we have given this information in brackets in every recipe to be clear.

Milk chocolate has the addition of milk powder. Look for one with at least 30% cocoa solids. I like a milk chocolate with caramel or malty notes.

White chocolate We don't use white chocolate in our chocolates and truffles. I find it too sweet. Providing it is made with only cocoa butter and no additional fats such as vegetable fat, then I regard it as chocolate and you'll find it used within our Patisserie, Ice Cream and Bars & Bites chapters.

Cocoa powder is made by pressing the cocoa butter out of the unsweetened cocoa mass. Natural cocoa powder has a red colour and can be quite acidic. Dutch-processed powder has been alkalized, has a milder flavour and a darker, red colour. I would generally recommend the latter variety, but always buy unsweetened cocoa powder with nothing artificial added.

Cocoa nibs are produced once the cocoa beans have been roasted and shelled and add a deep, crunchy flavour.

Shopping for Chocolate

Throughout this book we suggest using chocolate with a certain percentage of cocoa solids. This is just a guide and a way of showing you how we make the recipe in our shops. If you cannot get hold of a chocolate with the cocoa solid that the recipe suggests, or you would prefer a stronger or milder flavour, feel free to experiment – however, you must be aware that the outcome will be slightly different. Chocolate is temperamental by nature, and any slight change in the balance, will result in a different outcome, either for the better or for the worse. We would always recommend looking for quality couverture chocolate when you are cooking to this level.

When you are shopping for chocolate, here are a few pointers to look out for on the ingredients list:
• Please don't be influenced by the percentage of cocoa solids in a chocolate – it is not an indicator of quality, it is simply the combined content of cocoa mass and cocoa butter in the chocolate.
• Look for Trinitario or Criollo beans listed in the ingredients.
• Always avoid chocolates with lots of added ingredients, the purer the better.

Other Key Ingredients

Cream, butter and sugar are also key ingredients in chocolate making. We suggest using whipping (pouring) cream in virtually all of our recipes, but if you can't get hold of it, you can replace it with double (heavy) cream (the result will be slightly heavier). We use invert sugar *(see page 23)* in many recipes to stabilize the chocolate – if you can't get hold of this you can replace it with soft brown sugar.

Tasting Chocolate

I would recommend you take your time choosing chocolate to cook with. Buy small amounts of lots of varieties for tasting. Important flavours can often be very subtle and ultimately you will be able to enjoy eating chocolate more as you learn to identify different nuances of regions and blends and discover what aromas and qualities you love.

It has been said that there can be up to 400 aromas in one piece of chocolate, and these come from at least 300 chemical compounds. These can be wide and varied, from tobacco and malt to grass and fruits. Common aromas to detect are berries, honey, caramel, spices, citrus, vanilla, wine and mint.

Manufacturers who take pride in their blends will often include tasting notes on the bars as a reference for the consumer, but here is a guide to help you make the most of your senses in your tasting adventures:

Look The chocolate should be a deep mahogany brown. If it is near black then this is a sign of over-roasting. There shouldn't be any streaks from the chocolate blooming – this is either caused by fat bloom or sugar bloom, both of which are usually caused by quick changes in temperature or incorrect storage.

Listen A sure sign of good-quality chocolate is in the clean 'snap' when it is broken – it should not be crumbly at all.

Smell Good chocolate should have a complex fragrance, but it should not be over powering. It could smell sweet, fruity or nutty but not burnt, like chemicals or have no smell at all.

Taste When you first taste a chocolate you should place a piece on your tongue and allow it to melt slowly, letting the aromas fill your mouth. You will be able to taste natural elements, but also secondary elements that come with the roasting and blending of the beans. It is also important to acknowledge the aftertaste as a sign of good chocolate – it should linger, develop and have length.

Feel The chocolate should feel smooth in your mouth. Grainy chocolate is the sign of it being briefly conched or tempered badly, and sticky, claggy chocolate probably has had fats added to it instead of cocoa butter.

Storage & Longevity

All chocolate should be stored in a cool, dry and dark place as well as away from any powerful odours. Extreme temperatures and moisture will affect the chocolate and could be detrimental to your enjoyment of the products. Never put chocolate in the fridge as when it comes out to room temperature the condensation will bring moisture and cause sugar bloom.

We would suggest eating any chocolates you make within a few days – the fresher the better.

Commercial Kitchen vs Home Kitchen

This book has been designed to be an inspiration as well as a recipe book. It has taken over 20 years for me to gain these skills and the knowledge presented in this book. It offers a wide range of recipes and dishes to try at home, and as you develop your techniques your confidence will grow.

Our book contains the recipes we use in our kitchens and they have been adapted in the best way we can to be accessible and possible to recreate in your own homes. While we have done our utmost to make these recipes as home-kitchen-friendly as we can, you must remember that there are some fundamental differences between how you will make a product and how we will make it here in our kitchen.

A good example is when making ganaches we will always make the mixture, pipe or put it in a frame and leave it to set for 24 hours in a dehumidifying cabinet before dipping. Once the ganache chocolates are dipped we will then leave them again to set for a further 24 hours in the cabinet. This means that the produce will be stable enough for us to sell in our stores. However, when making chocolates at home it is up to you decide how long you leave your ganache to stabilize – if you're eating the chocolates that evening then you may not require such a long stabilization period.

With the patisserie we usually make all of the elements, such as sponges, glazes and syrups, in advance and in large batches, replenishing stock as we go. Then, when we require a finished product we will assemble all of the components together. You can of course take one or two of the components and create a simpler dish, which will still be delicious and look impressive.

You will notice in the photographs in this book that we often use pieces of equipment that you may not have in the home kitchen. Feel free to use alternative items (such as baking trays (sheets) instead of perspex sheets), but do be aware that the results may differ slightly due to the changes made.

CLASSIC TEMPERING

The cocoa butter in chocolate is made up of various fats that set at different temperatures, which makes the chocolate unstable. Tempering the chocolate encourages certain fats to form fat crystals that are stable and give a high gloss – this will bring the chocolate to an amalgamated crystalline state. Wrongly tempered chocolate will result in the chocolate setting badly (or with an unstable structure) and this causes fat bloom (seen as streaks on the surface and giving a crumbly texture) when it sets.

Chocolate tempered correctly, however, will set with a hard, protective surface, a good gloss and a brittle snap. It is vital that you always temper the chocolate before you coat your chocolates or prepare moulds or decorations. If the chocolate is streaky or dull, you will have to re-temper. It is possible that you did not meet some of the precise temperatres during the process.

500g (1lb 2oz) dark (bittersweet) chocolate (with 65% cocoa solids), finely chopped (or use chocolate chips)

1 Place the chopped chocolate into a porringer pot, double-boiler or over a bain-marie (water bath). Do not boil the water, as it may scald the chocolate. Stir regularly until the chocolate has melted. Continue to melt and stir until the chocolate reaches 45–50°C (113–122°F) ensuring all the fat and sugars have melted evenly.

2 Pour about two-thirds of the chocolate onto a marble or granite surface and leave the remaining chocolate in the porringer pot, double-boiler or over the bain-marie (water bath) to retain its temperature. The marble will help to cool the chocolate quickly.

Note:
• Be careful not to overheat, as you can scald the chocolate and it will become grainy and unstable.

3 Spread the melted chocolate back and forth with a step palette knife and a metal scraper, using firm sweeping movements and working gently so that no air gets incorporated. Continue this spreading process until the chocolate thickens and cools to about 28–29°C (82–84°F). You can check the temperature by using a thermometer, but be quick as the chocolate will thicken rapidly.

Tempering temperatures for Amedei Couverture

Chocolate	Melting temperature	Cooling temperature	Tempering temperature
Dark	45–50°C (113–122°F)	28–29°C (82–84°F)	31–32°C (88–90°F)
Milk	45–50°C (113–122°F)	26–27°C (79–81°F)	29–30°C (84–86°F)
White	45°C (113°F)	26–27°C (79–81°F)	29–30°C (84–86°F)

Our couverture chocolate of choice is Amedei *(see page 16)*. Temperatures that I state in the recipes are in line with using this brand of chocolate. Please note that other chocolate producers may have slightly different temperatures so it is always a good idea to experiment when trying out different brands of chocolate.

Tempering on a marble slab

Tempering on a marble (or granite) slab is popular in professional kitchens as the marble has great cooling qualities, even in the hottest of kitchens.

If you don't have a marble or granite work surface at home then it is best if you follow the seeded tempering method on pages 20–21.

4 Scrape the chocolate back into the porringer pot, double-boiler or over the bain-marie (water bath) and mix it with the remaining one-third of the melted chocolate until smooth.

5 The temperature should rise to 31–32°C (88–90°F). If the chocolate does not reach the correct temperature, warm the water slightly, stirring continuously.

Note: If the chocolate begins to cool and thickens while you are using it, simply warm the chocolate by reheating and stirring continuously. However, if you reheat too much it will lose it's temper.

Tempering Small Amounts

As a rough guide 500g (1lb 2oz) of tempered chocolate will coat about 80 chocolates. This is really the minimum amount of chocolate that you can temper. Therefore, all of our recipes specify this amount (unless a larger amount is needed), but you should be aware that there may be an amount of chocolate left over in the bowl. Leftover tempered chocolate should be poured into an airtight container, left to cool, then covered with the lid and stored in a cool, dry area for your next batch of tempering.

SEEDED TEMPERING

This is a great method as it requires no marble and it is very clean. All you will need is your porringer pot, double-boiler or bain-marie (water bath) and a thermometer. This is also the method I would suggest for tempering smaller batches. You will always need at least this amount for dipping and moulding.

500g (1lb 2oz) dark (bittersweet) chocolate (with 65% cocoa solids), finely chopped (or use chocolate chips)

1 Place two-thirds of the chopped chocolate into a porringer pot, double-boiler or over a bain-marie (water bath). Do not boil the water, as it may scald the chocolate. Stir regularly until the chocolate has completely melted and reaches 45–50°C (113–122°F) ensuring all the fat and sugars have melted evenly.

2 Gradually add the remaining chocolate – this is the seed. Stir vigorously and continue to stir until all of the chocolate has fully melted and the chocolate cools and thickens to 31–32°C (88–90°F) – keep checking using a thermometer. If the temperature drops below this, simply warm it up over the bain-marie again.

Tempering Tips

• When the chocolate reaches 31–32°C (88–90°F) this is known as the working temperature. The chocolate is tempered and ready to use. To test this manually, dip the end of a palette knife into the chocolate and allow to set. If the chocolate is smooth and glossy when set (see the right-hand knife opposite) you have successfully tempered your chocolate.

• Be very careful when using a bain-marie (water bath) that none of the water or steam escapes and gets into the chocolate. Chocolate is made up of cocoa solids, cocoa butter, sugar, vanilla and possibly milk powder. A small drop of water will moisten the ingredients and make the cocoa solids clump together and separate from the butter (in the same way that oil and water don't mix). You should never cover melting chocolate with a lid as the steam will condense and drop into the chocolate.

• If water or humidity gets into the chocolate it can still be used for ice cream or a chocolate drink as well as baking.

• Over heating separates the cocoa solids and other dry ingredients from the cocoa butter; it will begin to burn if over heated, the result being a dry, discoloured paste. There is no retrieving burnt chocolate, so be very careful when tempering.

BASIC GANACHE

Ganache is an emulsion of couverture chocolate and cream; however, other liquids can be also be added, such as fruit purée (see Blackcurrant Purée, page 124) to add a different flavour. It is the backbone for many of our chocolates and recipes throughout the book. The key to a good ganache is the quality of the ingredients – we use Amedei chocolate (see page 16),

a small Tuscan producer who make exceptional chocolate. We also source top-quality cream and butter and, equally important, fresh and natural ingredients, such as fresh rosemary and yuzu (a Japanese citrus fruit).

According to legend, ganache dates back to the late 19th century to a kitchen in France when a young apprentice chef,

while attempting to make crème anglaise, accidentally poured the hot cream into a bowl of chopped chocolate rather than his egg and sugar liaise. His chef called him a ganache, a fool in French. However, the young apprentice found that after mixing his cream and chocolate combination it became smooth and delicious, so not such a fool after all.

Makes enough for about 80 truffles or chocolates

435ml (14½fl oz/1¾ cups) whipping (pouring) cream
60g (2oz) invert sugar (see page 23)
500g (1lb 2oz) dark (bittersweet) chocolate (with 66% cocoa solids), finely chopped
75g (2½oz/6 tbsp) unsalted butter, cut into cubes and at room temperature

Demonstrated method
I have used this method now for many years and I find it to be the most stable for my chocolates.

1 Put the cream (or fruit purée – see Framboise Truffle, page 38) and invert sugar in a saucepan and bring to the boil. Take off the heat and leave to cool until it reaches 65–70°C (149–158°F).

2 Melt the chocolate in a bowl over a bain-marie (water bath) to about 45°C (113°F) and gradually add the cooled cream to the chocolate.

Alternative Method
using the same ingredients

1 Put the cream and invert sugar in a saucepan and bring to the boil.

2 Gradually add the cream to the chopped chocolate, mixing continuously to form an emulsion.

Invert Sugar

Invert sugar is sugar that has been through a process that inverts it's molecules. This can be done by heating a sugar and water solution, but is usually done with the addition of a catalyst to the syrup to speed up the process. It's useful for ganache as it can anti-crystallize and can set, absorb and stabilize the water and moisture in ganache, giving your products a naturally longer shelf-life. See the Directory on page 224 for stockists.

If you cannot get hold of invert sugar, the best substitute is soft brown sugar which you can substitute using the same quantities. The only difference will be that the shelf-life *(see page 19)* will diminish. Honey is another alternative, again substituted in the same quantities – however, it will bring honey flavours to your chocolates. You can also leave out the invert sugar all together, but the shelf-life will diminish, again meaning a quicker consumption is needed.

3 Mix continuously to form an emulsion.

4 Add the butter and continue to mix until fully incorporated. If you are adding any liquid to your ganache *(see page 35)*, add it now and mix well.

5 Leave the ganache to firm for about 1 hour and use as required.

3 Add the butter and continue to mix until fully incorporated.

4 Leave the ganache to firm for about 1 hour and use as required.

TRUFFLES

WHAT IS A TRUFFLE?

Truffles are, essentially, balls of ganache (see pages 22–23) – a mixture of chocolate, cream, sugar and butter that can also be used in filled chocolates and patisserie. The original chocolate truffle was a ball of ganache rolled in chocolate and cocoa powder. It was named after the precious black truffle fungus that it physically resembled. Over time, they have been flavoured with alcohol, fruits and nuts, but they traditionally retain a rustic appearance. We usually pipe our truffles in a variety of shapes and roll in various coatings, but always keep this rustic appearance. The only exception to this is the House Milk Truffle (see page 30), which we cut into squares.

All truffles should be stored in an airtight container in a cool, dry area (not in the fridge) and should be consumed within a few days (the fresher the better). If the quantities in these recipes are too high, feel free to halve the measurements.

Piping ganache

We use this piping method to make the majority of our truffles. It is incredibly easy to do and helps to give each truffle a rustic appearance.

3

4

5

1 Line a flat tray (sheet) with silicone (baking) paper and place a small amount of ganache in the corners of the tray underneath the paper. Press the paper down onto the ganache – this will prevent the paper from lifting when the ganache is piped.

2 Open a piping (pastry) bag, place a plain 12mm (½ inch) tube nozzle (tip) for bulbs and a plain 15mm (¾ inch) tube nozzle (tip) for the strips into the bag and cut the end of the bag to allow the nozzle (tip) through.

3 Half-fill the bag with the ganache – if you fill the bag too full it becomes more difficult to control.

4 Pipe 2cm (¾ inch) bulbs...

5 ... or finger-width strips of ganache onto the silicone (baking) paper leaving a small space between each one. Place the tray (sheet) in a cool, dry area and leave to set, uncovered, for 2–3 hours. You will then need to cut the strips using a warm, dry knife into 3.5cm (1½ inch) pieces.

Framing ganache

This method is generally used to make squares of ganache for our couture chocolates (see pages 42–83), but we do also use it to create our House Milk Truffles (see page 30).

1

2

3

1 Place a non-stick baking mat on a flat baking tray (sheet). Brush the mat with Chocolate Cocoa Butter Solution (see page 29) and leave to set for 4–5 minutes.

2 Pour a Basic Ganache (see pages 22–23) or your chosen flavoured or infused ganache (see pages 48–51) into the prepared baking mat.

3 Ensure the ganache spreads out evenly across the baking mat, place in a cool, dry area and leave to set, uncovered, overnight.

Cutting ganache

1 Using pastry wheels or a knife or skewer, score the surface of the ganache into 2.5cm (1 inch) squares. Heat a knife using a hairdryer (it is best to avoid doing it with hot water as the knife will be too wet).

2 Using the hot knife, cut the ganache along the scored lines into cubes.

1

2

4

5

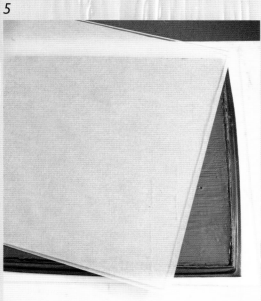

6

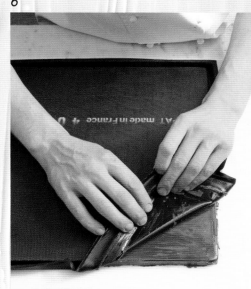

4 Brush the top of the set ganache with more chocolate cocoa butter solution and leave to set for 2–3 minutes.

5 Lay a sheet of silicone (baking) paper on top of the ganache. Place a baking tray (sheet) on top of that and, holding all three, carefully turn them over so that the tray is upturned.

6 Carefully peel away the non-stick baking mat and cut as desired (*see page 28*).

Chocolate Cocoa Butter Solution

Makes enough to brush about 3 trays (sheets)

60g (2oz) cocoa butter, finely chopped
120g (4¼oz) fine dark (bittersweet) chocolate (70% cocoa solids), finely chopped

Put the cocoa butter and chocolate in a bowl and melt gently over a bain-marie (water bath) until it reaches 45°C (113°F) on a thermometer. Leave it to cool slighty before using it to brush over non-stick baking mats as required. Leftover solution will keep in an airtight container for several months in a cool, dry area.

HOUSE DARK TRUFFLE

We have chosen two blends of chocolate as they work perfectly together for these truffles.

Makes about 80 truffles

I quantity **Basic Ganache** *(see pages 22–23)*, made with half fine dark (bittersweet) chocolate with 70% cocoa solids and half with 65% cocoa solids
500g (1lb 2oz) tempered fine dark (bittersweet) chocolate *(see pages 18–19)* and cocoa powder, to coat

1 Line a baking tray (sheet) with silicone (baking) paper. Spoon the basic ganache into a piping (pastry) bag fitted with a plain 15mm (¾ inch) nozzle (tip) and pipe finger-width rows onto the prepared tray (sheet). Leave to set, uncovered, overnight in a cool, dry area.

2 Use a warm, dry knife to cut the rows of ganache into 3.5cm (1½ inch) long oblongs.

3 Using a dipping fork, dip each ganache oblong into the tempered chocolate, ensuring it is evenly coated before removing it. Ease each truffle off the fork gently with a palette knife and place on a clean non-stick baking mat.

4 Put the cocoa powder in a shallow bowl or tray and roll each truffle in the powder until evenly coated. Remove from the cocoa powder and shake to eliminate any excess. Leave to set, uncovered, for 2–3 hours in a cool, dry area.

HOUSE MILK TRUFFLE

Rich, unadulterated and incredibly moreish truffles that are cut instead of piped for a different appearance.

Makes about 80 truffles

I quantity **Chocolate Cocoa Butter Solution** *(see page 29)*
300ml (½ pint/1¼ cups) whipping (pouring) cream
45g (1½oz) invert sugar *(see page 23)*
550g (1¼lb) fine milk chocolate (32% cocoa solids)

85g (3oz/7 tbsp) unsalted butter, cut into cubes and at room temperature
500g (1lb 2oz) tempered fine dark (bittersweet) chocolate *(see pages 18–19)* and cocoa powder, to coat

1 Place a non-stick baking mat on a baking tray (sheet) and brush the surface with the chocolate cocoa butter solution.

2 Put the cream and invert sugar in a saucepan and bring to the boil. Take off the heat and leave to cool until it reaches 65–70°C (149–158°F).

3 Melt the chopped chocolate in a bowl over a bain-marie (water bath) until it reaches about 45°C (113°F).

4 Gradually add the cooled cream to the chocolate, mixing continuously to form an emulsion. Add the butter and continue to mix until fully incorporated. Blend with a hand-held blender if necessary.

5 Pour the ganache into the prepared baking mat and leave to set overnight, uncovered, in a cool, dry area.

6 Brush the surface with some more chocolate cocoa butter solution, leave to set for 2–3 minutes and then cut into 2cm (¾ inch) squares with a warm, dry knife.

7 Using a dipping fork, dip each ganache square into the tempered chocolate, ensuring it is evenly coated before removing it. Ease each truffle off the fork gently with a palette knife and place on a sheet of silicone (baking) paper.

8 Put the cocoa powder in a shallow bowl or tray and roll each truffle in the powder until evenly coated. Remove from the cocoa powder and shake to eliminate any excess. Leave to set, uncovered, for 2–3 hours in a cool, dry area.

Right: A selection of truffles (from left): **House Dark**; **Yamazaki Single Malt Whisky** *(see page 35)*; **Framboise** *(see page 38)*; and **House Milk**.

MATCHA & PISTACHIO TRUFFLE

These truffles look fabulous and stand out in our chocolate cabinets. I am a huge fan of matcha (green tea powder) – it brings it's very own unique taste. Ideally, use Sicilian pistachio nuts as they have much more flavour.

Coating Truffles

Classically, truffles are coated in cocoa powder; however, we like to add a contemporary touch, giving our truffle range a little more variety. Texture plays an important part in our truffles, so using coatings such as the roasted Nutty Dacquoise (see pages 36–37), kinako powder with sesame seeds or dried hibiscus powder takes truffles to a whole new level.

Makes about 80 truffles

390ml (13fl oz/generous 1½ cups) whipping (pouring) cream
50g (1¾oz) invert sugar (see page 23)
10g (¼oz) matcha (green tea powder)
290g (10oz) fine milk chocolate (32% cocoa solids), finely chopped
190g (6½oz) fine dark (bittersweet) chocolate (63% cocoa solids), finely chopped
75g (2½oz) Pistachio Paste (see page 52)
60g (2oz/5 tbsp) unsalted butter, cut into cubes and at room temperature
500g (1lb 2oz) tempered fine dark (bittersweet) chocolate (see pages 18–19), to coat

For the matcha & pistachio coating:

8g (1¼ tsp) matcha (green tea powder)
250g (9oz/1⅔ cups) pistachios (dried out in a hot oven for 3–4 minutes), finely chopped

1 Line a baking tray (sheet) with silicone (baking) paper.

2 Put the cream and invert sugar in a saucepan and bring to the boil. Take off the heat and leave to cool until it reaches 65–70°C (149–158°F). Mix a little of the cream with the matcha powder to form a smooth paste.

3 Melt the chopped chocolate in a bowl over a bain-marie (water bath) to about 45°C (113°F) and gradually add the cooled cream to the chocolate. Continue to mix to form an emulsion. Mix in the pistachio paste and the matcha paste. Add the butter and continue to mix until fully incorporated. Blend with a hand blender if necessary.

4 Leave the ganache to firm for about 1 hour.

5 Spoon the ganache into a piping (pastry) bag fitted with a plain 12mm (½ inch) nozzle (tip) and pipe 2cm (¾ inch) bulbs onto the prepared tray (sheet). Leave to set, uncovered, for 2–3 hours in a cool, dry area.

6 To make the coating, mix together the matcha powder and finely chopped pistachios in a bowl and then place in a shallow bowl or tray.

7 Using a dipping fork, dip each ganache bulb in the tempered chocolate, ensuring it is evenly coated before removing it. Ease each truffle off the fork with a palette knife into the matcha and pistachio coating and roll to fully coat. Remove from the coating, shake to eliminate any excess and place on a clean non-stick baking mat. Leave to set, uncovered, for 2–3 hours in a cool, dry area.

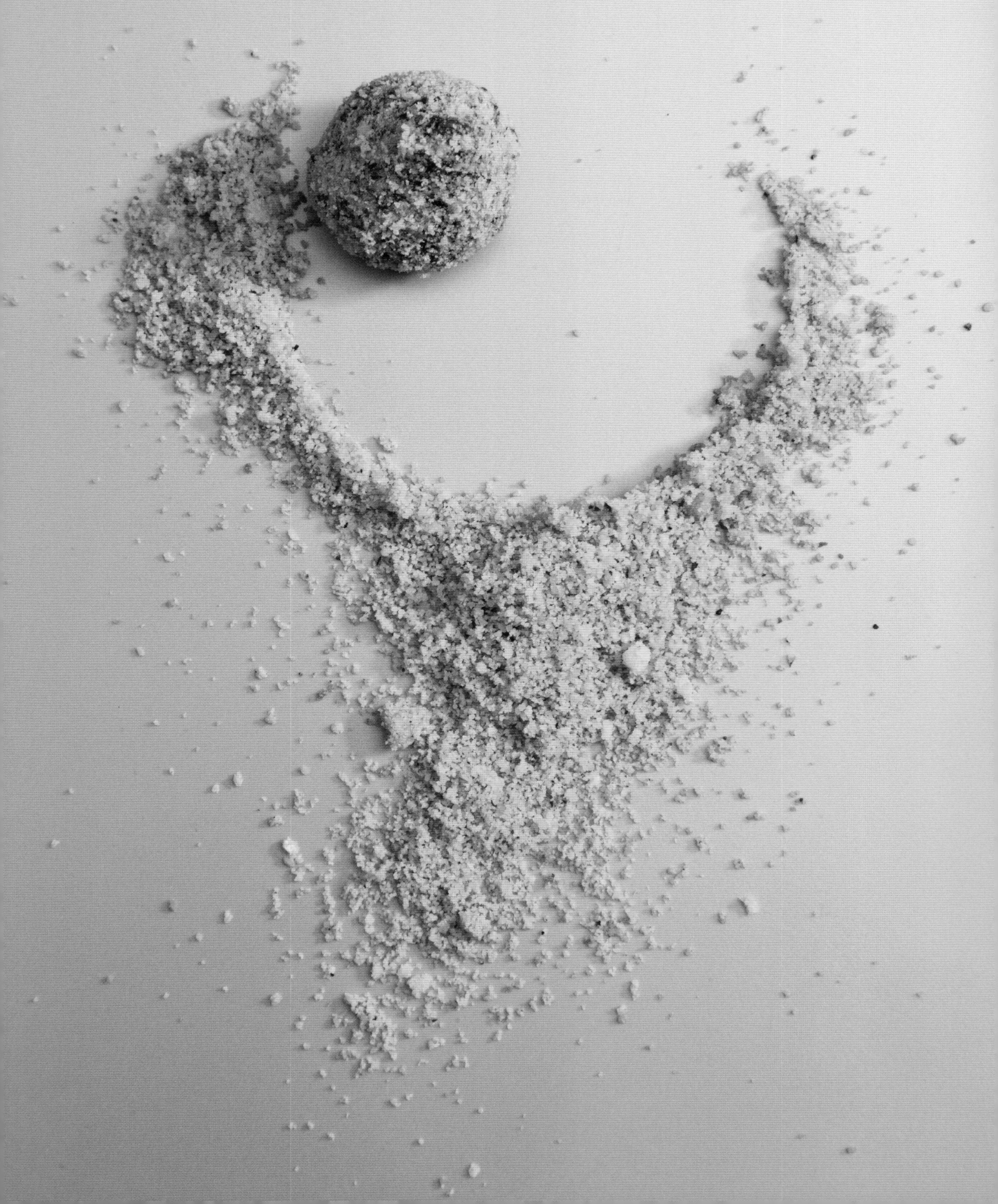

YAMAZAKI SINGLE MALT WHISKY & DACQUOISE TRUFFLE

This is a great combination, bringing Scotland and Japan together. The Yamazaki, delicate with vanilla and ripe fruit, works perfectly with the dark chocolate, and the coating brings another dimension with its crisp nutty notes.

Makes about 80 truffles

1 quantity **Basic Ganache** *(see pages 22–23)*, made with 100ml (3½fl oz/ generous ⅓ cup) Yamazaki single-malt whisky

½ quantity **Nutty Dacquoise** *(see pages 36–37)* and 500g (1lb 2oz) tempered fine dark (bittersweet) chocolate, to coat

1 Make the basic ganache following the method on pages 22–23, adding the whisky at step 4. Line a baking tray (sheet) with silicone (baking) paper.

2 Spoon the whisky ganache into a piping (pastry) bag fitted with a plain 12mm (½ inch) nozzle (tip) and pipe 2cm (¾ inch) bulbs onto the prepared tray (sheet). Leave to set, uncovered, for 2–3 hours in a cool, dry area.

3 Preheat the oven to 180°C (350°F/ Gas 4). Break the nutty dacquoise into pieces and place on a non-stick baking tray (sheet). Bake in the preheated oven for 6–8 minutes and then leave to cool. Transfer to a food processor and blitz to a crumb-like mixture. Place in a shallow dish or tray.

4 Using a dipping fork, dip each ganache bulb in the tempered chocolate, ensuring it is evenly coated before removing it. Ease each truffle off the fork with a palette knife into the dacquoise crumb and roll to fully coat. Remove from the coating, shake to eliminate any excess and place on a clean non-stick baking mat. Leave to set, uncovered, for 2–3 hours in a cool, dry area.

NUTTY DACQUOISE

This is a classic French meringue enriched with nuts and is used as a base in entremets *(see page 180)* to provide texture. We also use this for our Yamazaki Single Malt Whisky & Dacqouise Truffle *(see previous page)*, which gives a nutty crunchy coating.

**Makes enough to coat about
80 truffles**

65g (2¼oz/⅔ cup) chopped almonds
65g (2¼oz/⅔ cup) chopped hazelnuts
65g (2¼oz/¾ cup) ground almonds
65g (2¼oz/¾ cup) ground hazelnuts

125g (4½oz/¾ cup) icing (powdered/ pure) sugar, sifted
20g (¾oz) cornflour (cornstarch)
140g (5oz) egg whites (about 4½ eggs)
40g (1½oz) caster (superfine) sugar

1 Preheat the oven to 200°C (400°F/ Gas 6). Spread the chopped almonds and hazelnuts out on a non-stick baking tray (sheet). Spread the ground almonds and hazelnuts out on a separate baking tray (sheet). Lightly roast both trays of nuts in the preheated oven for 5–6 minutes and then leave to cool. Reduce the oven temperature to 180°C (350°F/Gas 4) and line a baking tray (sheet) with a non-stick baking mat.

2 Put the sifted icing (powdered or pure) sugar into a mixing bowl with the roasted ground nuts and cornflour (cornstarch). Mix together.

3 In a separate mixing bowl, slowly whisk the egg whites, then gradually increase the speed and add the caster (superfine) sugar. Continue to whisk to a firm meringue. Alternatively, whisk the egg whites in an electric mixer fitted with the whisk attachment.

4 Place the meringue into a large mixing bowl and fold in the icing (powdered or pure) sugar, ground nut and cornflour (cornstarch) mixture.

5 Fold in half of the roasted chopped nuts.

Storage Advice

Once the dacquoise has been baked and cooled and you have upturned it (*step 8 below*), wrap it in cling film (plastic wrap) and store it in the freezer until needed. If you are not planning on freezing it then it should ideally be used straightaway; however, it will keep for a couple of days in an airtight container if necessary.

6

7

8

6 Sprinkle the remaining chopped nuts over the prepared baking tray (sheet), and pour the meringue mixture on top of them.

7 Use a palette knife to level out the surface and bake in the preheated oven for 18–20 minutes. (If you will be using it for coating truffles, bake for a further 5 minutes.)

8 When cool, lay a sheet of silicone (baking) paper on top of the dacquoise. Place a baking tray (sheet) on top of that and holding all three, turn them over so that the tray is upturned. Remove the baking tray (sheet) on top and carefully peel away the non-stick baking mat.

9 For truffles, break the dacquoise into pieces and then blitz in a food processor and store in an airtight container until needed.

FRAMBOISE

Makes about 80 truffles

400g (14oz) ready-made raspberry purée (OR see **Blackcurrant Purée**, page 124)
60g (2oz) invert sugar (see page 23)
250g (9oz) fine dark (bittersweet) chocolate (63% cocoa solids), finely chopped
250g (9oz) fine dark (bittersweet) chocolate (66% cocoa solids), finely chopped
85g (3oz/7 tbsp) unsalted butter, cut into cubes and at room temperature
500g (1lb 2oz) tempered fine dark (bittersweet) chocolate (see pages 18–19) and cocoa powder, to coat

1 Line a baking tray (sheet) with silicone (baking) paper. Put the raspberry purée and invert sugar in a saucepan and bring to the boil. Take off the heat and leave to cool until it reaches 65–70°C (149–158°F).

2 Melt the chocolate over a bain-marie (water bath) to about 45°C (113°F) and gradually add the cooled raspberry mixture to the chocolate. Continue to mix to form an emulsion. Add the butter and continue to mix until fully incorporated. Blend with a hand blender if necessary. Leave the ganache to firm for about 1 hour.

3 Spoon the ganache into a piping (pastry) bag fitted with a plain 12mm (½ inch) nozzle (tip) and pipe 2cm (¾inch) bulbs onto the tray (sheet). Leave for 2–3 hours in a cool, dry area.

4 Using a dipping fork, dip each bulb into the tempered chocolate, ensuring it is evenly coated. Put the cocoa powder in a shallow bowl or tray and roll each truffle in the powder until evenly coated. Remove from the cocoa powder and shake to eliminate any excess. Leave to set, uncovered, for 2–3 hours in a cool, dry area.

JAPANESE SAKE & KINAKO

This truffle uses one of my favourite dry and fruity blends of Sake.

Makes about 80 truffles

1 quantity **Basic Ganache** (see pages 22–23), made with 100ml (3½fl oz/generous ⅓ cup) Kubota Senju (Japanese Sake)
250g (9oz/1⅔ cup) kinako powder (roasted ground soya beans, see page 224)
50g (1¾oz) black sesame seeds
500g (1lb 2oz) tempered fine dark (bittersweet) chocolate (see pages 18–19), to coat

1 Make the basic ganache following the method on pages 22–23, adding the sake at step 4. Line a baking tray (sheet) with silicone (baking) paper.

2 Spoon the Sake-flavoured ganache into a piping (pastry) bag fitted with a plain 12mm (½ inch) nozzle (tip) and pipe 2cm (¾ inch) bulbs onto the prepared tray (sheet). Leave to set for 2–3 hours in a cool, dry area.

3 Mix together the kinako and sesame seeds in a shallow bowl or tray. Using a dipping fork, dip each bulb into the tempered chocolate, ensuring it is evenly coated. Ease each truffle off the fork with a palette knife into the coating and roll to fully coat. Remove the truffles from the coating and shake to eliminate any excess. Leave to set, uncovered, for 2–3 hours in a cool, dry area.

Variation: Champagne

Follow the recipe above for Japanese Sake & Kinako, but replace the Sake with 175ml (6fl oz/generous ⅔ cup) Champagne and coat with Neige Décor (see page 218).

CASSIS & HIBISCUS

This truffle has been a favourite in the shop ever since Suzue created it.

Makes about 80 truffles

360g (12oz) **Blackcurrant Purée** (see page 124)
70g (2½oz) invert sugar (see page 23)
300g (10oz) fine dark (bittersweet) chocolate (70% cocoa solids), chopped
300g (10oz) fine milk chocolate (35% cocoa solids), finely chopped
100g (3½oz/1 stick) unsalted butter, cut into cubes and at room temperature
250g (9oz) Neige Décor (see page 218)
125g (4½oz) hibiscus flower powder (see page 224)
500g (1lb 2oz) tempered fine dark (bittersweet) chocolate (see pages 18–19)

1 Line a baking tray (sheet) with silicone (baking) paper. Put the blackcurrant purée and invert sugar in a saucepan, bring to the boil and then leave to cool to 65–70°C (149–158°F).

2 Melt the chocolate over a bain-marie (water bath) until it reaches 45°C (113°F). Gradually add the fruit mixture to the chocolate, mixing continuously to form an emulsion. Add the butter and mix until fully incorporated. Blend with a hand-held blender if necessary. Leave the ganache to firm for about 1 hour. Spoon the ganache into a piping (pastry) bag fitted with a plain 15mm (¾ inch) nozzle (tip) and pipe finger-width rows onto the lined tray. Leave to set for 2–3 hours. Use a warm, dry knife to cut the rows of ganache into 3.5cm (1½ inch) long oblongs.

3 Mix together the Neige Décor and hibiscus flower powder in a shallow bowl or tray. Using a dipping fork, dip each ganache oblong in the tempered chocolate, ensuring it is evenly coated. Ease each truffle off the fork into the coating and roll to fully coat. Leave to set for 2–3 hours.

Champagne

Cassis & Hibiscus

Framboise

Japanese Sake & Kinako

CHESTNUT & PRALINE

Not many of our truffles are dipped like this, but if you wanted to add a different texture to your truffles or chocolates, this recipe is good place to start.

Chestnut Purée

250g (9oz) vacuum-packed, cooked chestnuts
250ml (9fl oz/1 cup) milk
½ vanilla pod (bean), split lengthways

Put the chestnuts and milk in a saucepan. Scrape the seeds from the vanilla pod (bean) into the milk and drop in the empty pod too. Bring to the boil and cook over a low heat for 4–5 minutes. Remove the vanilla pod and leave to cool. Transfer to a bowl and blitz with a hand blender until smooth. Store in an airtight container in the fridge.

Makes about 80 truffles

330ml (11fl oz/1⅓ cups) whipping (pouring) cream
30g (1oz) invert sugar (see page 23)
125g (4½oz) chestnut purée (see box opposite)
380g (13oz) fine dark (bittersweet) chocolate (65% cocoa solids), finely chopped
125g (4½oz) fine milk chocolate (32% cocoa solids), finely chopped
225g (8oz) Praline Paste (see page 158)
50g (1¾oz/4 tbsp) unsalted butter, cut into cubes and at room temperature
100g (3½oz) roasted nibbed almonds (or roasted almonds cut into strips) and 500g (1lb 2oz) tempered fine dark (bittersweet) chocolate (see pages 18–19), to coat

1 Line a baking tray (sheet) with silicone (baking) paper.

2 Put the cream and invert sugar in a saucepan and bring to the boil. Take off the heat, mix in the chestnut purée and leave to cool until it reaches 65–70°C (149–158°F).

3 Melt the chocolate in a bowl over a bain-marie (water bath) until it reaches about 45°C (113°F) and gradually add the cooled chestnut cream to the chocolate. Continue to mix to form an emulsion. Mix in the praline paste, add the butter and continue to mix until fully incorporated. Leave the ganache to firm for about 1 hour.

4 Spoon the ganache into a piping (pastry) bag fitted with a plain 12mm (½ inch) nozzle (tip) and pipe 2cm (¾ inch) bulbs onto the prepared tray (sheet). Leave to set for 2–3 hours in a cool, dry area.

5 Mix the roasted almonds with the tempered chocolate. Using a dipping fork, dip each ganache bulb into the chocolate coating, ensuring it is evenly coated before removing it. Ease each truffle off the fork with a palette knife onto a sheet of silicone (baking) paper and leave to fully set for about 1 hour in a cool, dry area.

COUTURE
CHOCOLATES

MAKING A COUTURE CHOCOLATE

Our couture chocolates epitomize our business philosophy. They are tailor-made, fresh and natural. Alongside all of our products, they contain no artificial preservatives, which although means they don't have a substantial shelf-life, it does mean that they are of the highest quality.

Using infusions to subtly flavour the ganaches means that we get the real flavour and do not need to use oils or essences and the chocolate can reach its full potential – being as enjoyable as possible without being full of unnecessary ingredients.

The term 'couture' evokes images of high-end, custom-made products and luxury, all ideals we believe represent our brand. We strive to give those who devour our chocolates an experience – something extraordinary and exciting.

This chapter is structured to first show you the chocolate-making skills and techniques that you will need to use, followed by the recipes.

Clockwise from top left:
Piedmont Hazelnut; **Szechuan Pepper**; **Chauo**; **Pistachio Toscano**; **Juniper Berry & Blackcurrant**; **Raspberry & Toscano**; and **Passion Fruit & Mango**.

1 Brush a non-stick baking mat with Chocolate Cocoa Butter Solution (see page 29).

2 Make an infused or flavoured ganache (see pages 48–51) and pour it into the prepared mat. Level out the surface and leave to set overnight in a cool, dry area.

3 Brush the ganache with more chocolate cocoa butter solution; leave to set for 2–3 minutes.

4 Lay a sheet of silicone (baking) paper on top of the ganache. Place an acrylic sheet or baking tray (sheet) on top of that and, holding all three, carefully turn them over so that the tray (sheet) is upturned.

5 Carefully peel away the non-stick baking mat.

6 Score and cut the ganache following the instructions on page 28.

7 Secure each chocolate on a dipping fork and dip in tempered chocolate. Tap to shake off any excess and place on silicone (baking) paper. Decorate as desired (see pages 58–61).

To make an infused or flavoured ganache chocolate

1

2

3

4

5

6

7

Baking Trays (sheets)
Our recipes make about 80 chocolates using a 25.5 × 30cm (10 × 12 inch) non-stick baking mat with sides. Use as close to this size as possible, but make sure it has a depth of at least 1.5cm (¾ inch).

To make a layered chocolate

1. Brush a non-stick baking mat with Chocolate Cocoa Butter Solution *(see page 29)*.

2. Make your chosen layer *(see Feuillantine, pages 54–55 or Pistachio Marzipan, pages 52–53)* and spread it into the prepared baking mat. Smooth out the surface and trim the edges if necessary so that it sits neatly within the mat.

3. Make a half quantity of the Basic Ganache *(see pages 22–23)* and pour it over the layer. Level out the surface and leave to set overnight in a cool, dry area.

4. Brush the ganache with more chocolate cocoa butter solution; leave to set for 2–3 minutes.

5. Lay a sheet of silicone (baking) paper on top of the ganache. Place an acrylic sheet or baking tray (sheet) on top of that.

6. Holding all three, carefully turn them over so that the tray (sheet) is upturned. Carefully peel away the non-stick baking mat.

7. Score and cut the ganache following the instructions on page 28.

8. Secure each chocolate on a dipping fork and dip in tempered chocolate. Tap to shake off any excess and place on silicone (baking) paper. Decorate as desired *(see pages 58–61)*.

To make a jelly-layered chocolate

1 Make your chosen jelly layer *(see Pâté de Fruits, pages 56–57 or other flavour variations, page 74)* and spread it into a non-stick baking mat. Smooth out the surface and leave to set overnight in a cool, dry area.

2 Make a half quantity of the Basic Ganache *(see pages 22–23)* and pour it over the set jelly. Level out the surface and leave to set overnight in a cool, dry area.

3 Brush the ganache with more chocolate cocoa butter solution; leave to set for 2–3 minutes.

4 Lay a sheet of silicone (baking) paper on top of the ganache. Place an acrylic sheet or baking tray (sheet) on top of that and, holding all three, carefully turn them over so that the tray (sheet) is upturned.

5 Carefully peel away the non-stick baking mat — the jelly layer will now be on top.

6 Brush the jelly surface with more chocolate cocoa butter solution and leave to set for 2–3 minutes.

7 Score and cut the ganache following the instructions on page 28.

8 Secure each chocolate on a dipping fork and dip in tempered chocolate. Tap to shake off any excess and place on silicone (baking) paper. Decorate as desired *(see pages 58–61)*.

MAKING INFUSED GANACHE

Tarragon & Mustard Ganache *(see also page 70)*
This is a daring combination — the chocolate aniseed notes work with the woodland notes of the tarragon, with the mustard adding a little warmth.

Why we infuse

Traditionally chocolates in the UK have a long shelf-life, with additives and flavourings, but for us it's about keeping the chocolates pure. If we are making a mint chocolate we use fresh mint to infuse the cream to get its wonderful flavour rather than a potion or oil, for example.

You can add different flavours to chocolate ganache. Fresh herbs, such as fresh rosemary, tarragon, shiso and lemon thyme, can be infused in the cream that is used for the ganache (see step-by-step instructions). They are then strained off to leave a flavoured cream. Teas and spices such as Jasmine, Szechuan pepper and lemongrass and ginger can also be infused in the same way, though they need to be left in the cream for longer. For other flavourings, such as toasted sesame, Japanese black vinegar and honey, for example, the ingredients can be added directly to the ganache.

Makes enough for about 80 chocolates

400ml (14fl oz/1⅔ cups) whipping (pouring) cream
20g (¾oz) tarragon
60g (2oz) invert sugar *(see page 23)*
4.5g (¾ tsp) mustard powder

450g (1lb) fine dark (bittersweet) chocolate (66% cocoa solids), finely chopped
70g (2½oz/6 tbsp) unsalted butter, cut into cubes and at room temperature

1 Put the cream in a saucepan and bring to the boil. Add the tarragon.

2 Turn the heat off and cover the saucepan with cling film (plastic wrap). Leave it to cool and infuse for 2 hours.

3 Pass the infused cream through a fine sieve (strainer) to catch the tarragon.

4 Carefully press the tarragon in the sieve (strainer) with a ladle to squeeze as much of the flavour from the herb as possible.

Tarragon & Mustard Ganache
continued

> ### Sugar, Salt & Butter
> I'm very aware of the bad reputation sugar, salt and butter often get lumbered with. While I would agree that these are unhealthy in excess, they are all very important, natural ingredients in a pastry kitchen. They not only provide flavour, but are often essential to the success of a recipe and it would be impossible to create great patisserie and chocolates without them.

5 | 6 | 7

5 Return the cream to the saucepan. Add the invert sugar and bring to the boil again. Take off the heat. Pour off a little of the infused cream into a bowl with the mustard powder and mix until smooth.

6 Return the mustard paste to the cream in the pan.

7 Leave the cream to cool until it reaches 65–70°C (149–158°F).

8 Melt the chocolate over a bain-marie (water bath) to about 45°C (113°F) and gradually add the cooled cream to the chocolate, mixing continuously to form an emulsion. Add the butter and continue to mix until smooth. Leave the ganache to firm for about 1 hour either in the bowl or pour into a frame for cutting later *(see page 28)*.

8

LAYERING PISTACHIO MARZIPAN

I enjoy bringing great combinations together – marzipan and chocolate work well together and the Sicilian pistachios are full of flavour. The texture of the nutty marzipan with a fruity ganache (see page 64 for the full recipe) is a winning combination.

Pistachio Marzipan

Makes enough for about 80 chocolates

1 quantity **Chocolate Cocoa Butter Solution** *(see page 29)*
425g (15oz) marzipan
50g (1¾oz/⅓ cup) pistachios,
 roughly chopped
½ quantity **Basic Ganache**
 (see pages 22–23)

Icing (powdered/pure) sugar, to dust

For the pistachio paste
100g (3½oz/⅔ cup) pistachios
15ml (3 tsp) pistachio oil
 (or another flavourless nut oil)

1 Brush a non-stick baking mat with a thin layer of the chocolate cocoa butter solution. To make the pistachio paste, put the pistachios and oil in a food processor or blender (we recommend a Thermomix, *see page 224*) and blitz together until it becomes a smooth paste.

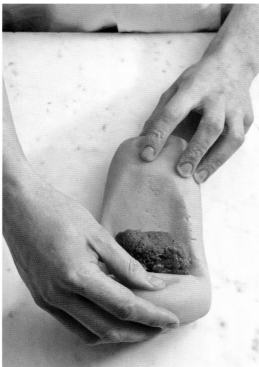

2 Make a cavity in the marzipan and spoon in the pistachio paste. Knead the marzipan until the paste is completely mixed in and the marzipan is smooth.

3 Add the chopped pistachios to the marzipan.

4 Knead again until the pistachios are fully incorporated. Roll into a sausage shape. Roll the marzipan out until it is 6mm (¼ inch) thick on a work surface lightly dusted with icing (powdered/pure) sugar.

5 Use the rolling pin to lift up the sheet of marzipan into the prepared baking mat. Trim the edges so that it sits neatly.

6 Pour over the chocolate ganache and leave to set. Continue with steps 4–8 of how to make a layered chocolate on page 46.

FEUILLANTINE BASE

These dried and crushed wafers mixed with our praline, Piedmont hazelnuts and milk chocolate give the most fabulous flavour to our chocolates. Be careful not to over-work the mixture, otherwise you will lose some of the texture. Almonds or walnuts also work well.

Makes enough for about 80 chocolates

1 quantity **Chocolate Cocoa Butter Solution** *(see page 29)*
130g (4½oz) fine milk chocolate (35% cocoa solids), finely chopped
75g (2½oz) gianduja *(see pages 218– 219)*, finely chopped
140g (5oz) **Praline Paste** *(see pages 158–159)*

25g (scant 1oz/2 tbsp) sea salt butter, cut into cubes and at room temperature
90g (3oz/scant 1 cup) chopped Piedmont hazelnuts, chopped
115g (4oz) feuillantine wafers

2

3

4

1 Brush a non-stick baking mat with the chocolate cocoa butter solution until it is evenly covered.

2 Melt the milk chocolate and gianduja in a bowl over a bain-marie (water bath) until it reaches 45°C (113°F). Mix in the praline paste.

3 Leave to cool to 37–38°C (99– 100°F). Add the butter and continue to mix until fully incorporated. Blend with a hand blender if necessary.

4 Add the Piedmont hazelnuts to the chocolate and mix well.

5 Add in the feuillantine wafers.

6 Mix until fully incorporated and then spread the mixture into the prepared baking mat using a palette knife.

7 Continue with steps 3–8 of how to make a layered chocolate on page 46.

PÂTÉ DE FRUITS

The region of Auvergne in south-west France is famed for Pâté de Fruits and it dates back to the 17th century. Although the recipe has evolved it is still as it translates a fruit paste, traditionally cut into cubes and rolled in sugar. We use our Pâté de Fruits to complement our chocolate ganache in a selection of our couture chocolates – the sharpness of the Pâté de Fruits works wonderfully with our smooth ganache.

This recipe is for a Raspberry Pâté de Fruits, but feel free to experiment with different fruits to get different flavours (see page 74 for some other flavour inspiration) – just replace the raspberry purée and fruit with another fruit.

Makes enough for about 80 chocolates

280g (10oz) ready-made raspberry purée
  (OR see **Blackcurrant Purée**, page 124)
50g (1¾oz) raspberries
225g (8oz/1 cup) caster (superfine) sugar
95g (3½oz) liquid glucose
10g (¼oz) yellow pectin
2.5ml (½ tsp) lemon juice

2

3

1 Put the raspberry purée, raspberries, 150g (5½oz/⅔ cup) of the caster (superfine) sugar and the liquid glucose in a saucepan and bring to the boil.

2 Mix together the pectin and the remaining sugar in a small bowl and add to the boiled raspberry liquid.

3 Cook over a low heat, mixing continuously until it reaches 103°C (217°F) on a sugar thermometer and mix in the lemon juice.

4 Pour the raspberry mixture into a non-stick baking mat and leave to set overnight in a cool, dry area.

5 Continue with steps 3–8 of how to make a jelly-layered chocolate on page 47.

Note: you could also pour into a shallow baking tray (sheet), leave to set, cut and then roll in granulated (white) sugar and enjoy on its own.

SPRINKLING & DECORATING

We like to decorate our chocolates partly so you can identify them from one another, but also to give them their own personal touch. We take care with every chocolate, placing each decoration by hand, and this is why we feel it is so important to take time over this stage of the process.

1 Using a dipping fork, dip each ganache cube in some tempered chocolate and ensure it is evenly coated.

2 Tap the fork on the side of the bowl/pot to remove any excess chocolate.

Top row, left to right: basil and sea salt; matcha (green tea powder); green tea; and freshly ground cardamom. *Middle row, left to right:* dried ginger; dried yuzu (Japanese citrus fruit); cocoa nibs; and sesame seeds. *Bottom row, left to right:* houji cha (smoked tea leaves); hibiscus powder; bramble and sea salt; and black mustard seeds.

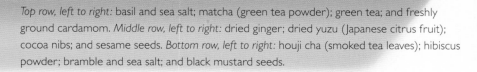

3 Top each chocolate with a sprinkle of your chosen decoration...

4 ...or place your decoration on top of the chocolate if it is something other than a powder or grating.

5 Leave to set for about 2 hours in a cool, dry area.

Top to bottom: lavender; rosemary and sea salt; Thai basil; pistachio; and gold leaf.

DECORATING WITH PERFORATING

A simple and effective way of creating a textured finish on our couture chocolates.

1 Using a dipping fork, dip each ganache cube in some tempered chocolate and ensure it is evenly coated.

2 Tap the fork on the side of the bowl/pot to remove any excess chocolate. Leave to set.

3 Perforate the top of each chocolate with a clean, dry knife or other utensil of choice to create a pattern or mark. You could use a marked knife or a shaped cutter, for example.

4 Leave to set for about 2 hours in a cool, dry area.

Coating Chocolates

Coating your chocolate protects the centre, which would dry up quickly if uncoated. It also adds a thin crisp layer, enhancing its characteristics. I would suggest using medium balanced chocolate and avoid using one with strong flavours as it will not work with the centres. We use Amedei blend 63 or 65 – both are balanced chocolates with a very smooth round finish and no bitter notes or acid. You can try various chocolates to see what works best for you.

2

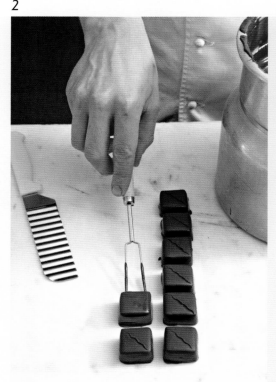

3

DECORATING WITH EMBOSSING

Embossing with acetate gives a unique, shiny textural finish.

1 Using a dipping fork, dip each ganache cube in some tempered chocolate and ensure it is evenly coated.

2 Tap the fork on the side of the bowl/pot to remove any excess chocolate.

3 Turn each chocolate over and place on a sheet of embossed acetate that will create a pattern on the base. Leave to set for about 2 hours in a cool, dry place.

Note: if you cannot get hold of any embossed acetate *(see Directory, page 224)* you can use patterned florist paper as an alternative or anything patterned lying around at home as long as it's had a good clean before using.

3

Chocolate Tips
- Allowing the ganache to dry out and set overnight helps the chocolate when you are coating it as it will stick better.
- The ideal temperature for your kitchen while you are making chocolates is around 24°C (75°F) – if it is any cooler than this the chocolate will set quicker, making it harder to decorate.
- The perfect temperature for a cool, dry area is around 12–15°C (54–59°F) – this is where you should leave your chocolate to set overnight.

The Chocolates

Top to bottom:
Couture Chocolates with Nuts & Seeds
Piedmont Hazelnut;
Chuao;
Coffee & Walnut;
Toasted Sesame;
and Pistachio & Toscano.

COUTURE CHOCOLATES WITH NUTS & SEEDS

Piedmont Hazelnut

This chocolate uses the crème de la crème of hazelnuts sourced from the Piedmont region in northern Italy.

Makes about 80 chocolates

1 quantity Feuillantine Base
   (see pages 54–55)
1 quantity Chocolate Cocoa Butter
   Solution *(see page 29)*
500g (1lb 2oz) tempered fine dark
   (bittersweet) chocolate
   (see pages 18–19), to coat

For the gianduja ganache
160ml (5fl oz/⅔ cup) whipping
   (pouring) cream
¼ vanilla pod (bean), split lengthways
20g (¾oz) invert sugar *(see page 23)*
115g (4oz) gianduja *(see pages 218–219)*
115g (4oz) fine dark (bittersweet)
   chocolate (65% cocoa solids), chopped
25g (scant 1oz/2 tbsp) unsalted butter,
   cut into cubes and at room temperature

1 Make the feuilletine base and use it to line a non-stick baking mat as instructed on pages 54–55.

2 To make the ganache, put the cream in a saucepan. Scrape the vanilla seeds from the split pod (bean) into the cream and drop in the empty pod. Bring to the boil. Take off the heat, cover with cling film (plastic wrap) and leave to infuse for 1 hour. Pass the infused cream through a fine sieve (strainer) to catch the vanilla pod. Return the cream to the saucepan, add the invert sugar and bring to the boil again. Take off the heat and leave to cool until it reaches 65–70°C (149–158°F).

3 Melt the gianduja and chocolate over a bain-marie (water bath) to about 45°C (113°F) and gradually add the cooled cream to the chocolate. Continue to mix to form an emulsion. Add the butter and continue to mix until fully incorporated. Blend with a hand blender if necessary.

4 Pour the ganache on top of the feuillantine base and leave to set overnight in a cool, dry area.

5 Brush the surface with chocolate cocoa butter solution and then continue with steps 5–8 of how to make a layered chocolate on page 46.

6 Decorate by pressing the wide end of a small piping nozzle into the chocolate to create a circular pattern. Leave to fully set for about 2 hours in a cool, dry area.

Pistachio & Toscano

The pistachio balances the rich chocolate.

Makes about 80 chocolates

1 quantity Chocolate Cocoa Butter
   Solution *(see page 29)*
1 quantity Pistachio Marzipan
   (see pages 52–53)
240ml (8fl oz/scant 1 cup) whipping
   (pouring) cream
30g (1oz) invert sugar *(see page 23)*
275g (9½oz) fine dark (bittersweet)
   chocolate (70% cocoa solids),
   finely chopped
40g (1½oz/3 tbsp) unsalted butter, cut
   into cubes and at room temperature
500g (1lb 2oz) tempered fine dark
   (bittersweet) chocolate
   (see pages 18–19), to coat
Sliced Sicilian pistachios, to decorate

1 Line a baking tray (sheet) with a non-stick baking mat and brush it liberally with the chocolate cocoa butter solution. Leave to set for 4–5 minutes. Use the pistachio marzipan to line the mat following the instructions on pages 52–53. Trim it to fit and neaten the edges.

2 Put the cream and invert sugar in a saucepan and bring to the boil. Take off the heat and leave to cool until it reaches 65–70°C (149–158°F).

3 Melt the chocolate in a bowl over a bain-marie (water bath) to about 45°C (113°F) and gradually add the cooled cream to the chocolate. Continue to mix to form an emulsion. Add the butter and continue to mix until fully incorporated. Blend with a hand blender if necessary.

4 Pour the ganache on top of the marzipan and leave to set overnight in a cool, dry area.

5 Brush the surface with chocolate cocoa butter solution and then continue with steps 5–8 of how to make a layered chocolate on page 46.

6 Decorate with the sliced pistachios and leave to fully set for about 2 hours in a cool, dry area.

Coffee & Walnut

This is one of my favourite cake combinations. Here we use the walnuts in the crunchy base.

Makes about 80 chocolates

1 quantity **Feuillantine Base** *(see pages 54–55)*, made by replacing the hazelnuts with 90g (3oz/1 cup) chopped walnuts
180ml (6fl oz/¾ cup) whipping (pouring) cream
3g (½ tsp) freshly ground coffee
30g (1oz) invert sugar *(see page 23)*
200g (7oz) fine dark (bittersweet) chocolate (70% cocoa solids), chopped
30g (1oz/2 tbsp) unsalted butter, cut into cubes and at room temperature
1 quantity **Chocolate Cocoa Butter Solution** *(see page 29)*
500g (1lb 2oz) tempered fine dark (bittersweet) chocolate *(see pages 18–19)*, to coat
Finely chopped coffee beans, to decorate

1 Make the feuillantine base (adding in 100g (3½oz) chopped walnuts) and use it to line a non-stick baking mat as instructed on pages 54–55.

2 Put the cream in a saucepan and bring to the boil. Add the coffee, then take off the heat, cover with cling film (plastic wrap) and leave to infuse for 2 hours.

3 Pass the infused cream through a fine sieve (strainer) to catch the coffee and return the cream to the saucepan. Add the invert sugar and bring to the boil again. Take off the heat and leave to cool until it reaches 65–70°C (149–158°F).

4 Melt the chocolate in a bowl over a bain-marie (water bath) to about 45°C (113°F) and gradually add the cooled cream to the chocolate. Continue to mix to form an emulsion. Add the butter and continue to mix until fully incorporated. Blend with a hand-held blender if necessary.

5 Pour the infused ganache on top of the feuillantine base and leave to set overnight in a cool, dry area.

6 Brush the surface with chocolate cocoa butter solution and then continue with steps 5–8 of how to make a layered chocolate on page 46.

7 Decorate by sprinkling with the chopped coffee beans and leave to fully set for about 2 hours in a cool, dry area.

Chuao

Makes about 80 chocolates

1 quantity **Chocolate Cocoa Butter Solution** *(see page 29)*
400ml (14fl oz/1⅔ cups) whipping (pouring) cream
60g (2oz) invert sugar *(see page 23)*
450g (1lb) Chuao chocolate *(see pages 218–219)*, finely chopped
70g (2½oz/6 tbsp) unsalted butter, cut into cubes and at room temperature
500g (1lb 2oz) tempered fine dark (bittersweet) chocolate *(see pages 18–19)*, to coat
Edible gold leaf, to decorate

1 Line a baking tray (sheet) with a non-stick baking mat and brush it liberally with the chocolate cocoa butter solution.

2 Put the cream and invert sugar in a saucepan and bring to the boil. Take off the heat and leave to cool until it reaches 65–70°C (149–158°F).

3 Melt the chocolate in a bowl over a bain-marie (water bath) to about 45°C (113°F) and gradually add the cooled cream to the chocolate. Continue to mix to form an emulsion. Add the butter and continue to mix until fully incorporated. Blend with a hand-held blender if necessary.

4 Pour the ganache into the mat and leave to set overnight in a cool, dry area.

5 Brush the surface with chocolate cocoa butter solution and then continue with steps 4–7 of how to make a flavoured ganache chocolate on page 45.

6 Decorate with some edible gold leaf and leave to fully set for about 2 hours in a cool, dry area.

Flavour Variations

Toasted Sesame
Follow the Chuao recipe but use 420g (15oz) fine dark (bittersweet) chocolate (65% cocoa solids) and 60g (2oz) gianduja instead of the Chuao chocolate. Also add 10g (¼oz) ready-made white sesame paste (see page 224) and 10g (¼oz) ready-made black sesame paste *(see page 224)* after you have added the butter to the ganache. Decorate with some toasted white sesame seeds.

SPICY COUTURE CHOCOLATES

Lemongrass & Ginger

Spices and chocolate are a great combination; there are so many varieties available you need never run out of ideas. Be careful to follow the recipes carefully, particularly when weighing out the spices. As with all of our chocolates we add the spice as a subtle note, letting it season the ganache and encourage the flavours out of the chocolate.

Makes about 80 chocolates

1 quantity of Chocolate Cocoa Butter
   Solution *(see page 29)*
400ml (14fl oz/1⅔ cups) whipping
   (pouring) cream
10g (¼oz) fresh lemongrass,
   roughly chopped
2.5g (½ tsp) grated fresh root ginger
60g (2oz) invert sugar *(see page 23)*
450g (1lb) fine dark (bittersweet)
   chocolate (63% cocoa solids),
   finely chopped
60g (2oz/5 tbsp) unsalted butter, cut into
   cubes and at room temperature
500g (1lb 2oz) tempered fine dark
   (bittersweet) chocolate
   (see pages 18–19), to coat
Dried fresh root ginger
   (see box, page 68), to decorate

1 Line a baking tray (sheet) with a non-stick baking mat and brush it liberally with the chocolate cocoa butter solution.

2 Put the cream in a saucepan and bring to the boil. Add the lemongrass and ginger, then take off the heat, cover with cling film (plastic wrap) and leave to infuse for 4 hours.

3 Pass the infused cream through a fine sieve (strainer) to catch the lemongrass and ginger. Return the cream to the saucepan, add the invert sugar and bring to the boil again. Take off the heat and leave to cool until it reaches 65–70°C (149–158°F).

4 Melt the chocolate in a bowl over a bain-marie (water bath) to about 45°C (113°F) and gradually add the cooled cream to the chocolate. Continue to mix to form an emulsion. Add the butter and continue to mix until fully incorporated. Blend with a hand blender if necessary.

5 Pour the infused ganache into the prepared baking mat and leave to set overnight in a cool, dry area.

6 Brush the surface with chocolate cocoa butter solution and then continue with steps 4–7 of how to make an infused or flavoured ganache chocolate on page 45.

7 Decorate by sprinkling with the dried ginger and leave to fully set for about 2 hours in a cool, dry area.

Spice Variations

Szechuan Pepper
Follow the recipe above, but replace the lemongrass and ginger with 6g (1 tsp) Szechuan pepper and use 425g (15oz) fine dark (bittersweet) chocolate (66% cocoa solids) and 65g (2¼oz) gianduja *(see pages 218–219)*. Sprinkle with dried Szechuan pepper powder *(see box, page 68)* to decorate.

Cardamom
Follow the recipe above, but replace the lemongrass and ginger with 15g (½oz) cardamom (pods crushed and husks removed). Use some wire mesh to decorate *(see pages 60–61)*.

Star Anise
Follow the recipe above, but replace the lemongrass and ginger with 6g (scant ¼oz) star anise and use 450g (1lb) fine dark (bittersweet) chocolate (63% cocoa solids) and 50g (1¾oz) gianduja *(see pages 218–219)*. Decorate by sprinkling with some dried aniseed powder *(see box, page 68)*.

Top to bottom:
Spicy Couture Chocolates
Lemongrass & Ginger;
Szechuan Pepper;
Cardamom;
and Star Anise.

COUTURE CHOCOLATES WITH SWEET HERBS

Rosemary & Olive Oil

This chocolate was a turning point for lots of our more traditional customers. It is one of our more accessible flavours and is a good bridge between the classic and the contemporary. It works best with a peppery olive oil.

Makes about 80 chocolates

1 quantity Chocolate Cocoa Butter
   Solution *(see page 29)*
400ml (14fl oz/1⅔ cups) whipping
   (pouring) cream
4g (⅔ tsp) rosemary sprigs
60g (2oz) invert sugar *(see page 23)*
2g (1/4 tsp) sea salt
450g (1lb) fine dark (bittersweet)
   chocolate (66% cocoa solids),
   finely chopped
15g (½oz/1 tbsp) unsalted butter, cut
   into cubes and at room temperature
75ml (2½fl oz/scant ⅓ cup) olive oil
500g (1lb 2oz) tempered fine dark
   (bittersweet) chocolate
   (see pages 18–19), to coat
Dried rosemary strips *(see box)*,
   to decorate

Dried decorations

To dry the rosemary above, wash the rosemary and remove the sprigs. Using a sharp knife cut fine strips from the rosemary leaves. Blanch in boiling water, refresh in cold water and drain and dry on paper towels. Put the rosemary strips on a non-stick baking mat and dry in the oven on its lowest setting (100°C/212°F/Gas 1/4 with the oven door slightly ajar) for 2 hours or until dry. Store any unused dried herb in an airtight container. Use this process with other herbs to create different flavours.

1 Line a baking tray (sheet) with a non-stick baking mat and brush it liberally with the chocolate cocoa butter solution.

2 Put the cream in a saucepan and bring to the boil. Add the rosemary, then take off the heat, cover with cling film (plastic wrap) and leave to infuse for 2 hours.

3 Pass the infused cream through a fine sieve (strainer) to catch the rosemary. Return the cream to the saucepan, add the invert sugar and salt and bring to the boil again. Take off the heat and leave to cool until it reaches 65–70°C (149–158°F).

4 Melt the chocolate in a bowl over a bain-marie (waer bath) to about 45°C (113°F) and gradually add the cooled cream to the chocolate. Continue to mix to form an emulsion. Add the butter and continue to mix until fully incorporated. Gradually add the olive oil and mix until smooth. Blend with a hand blender if necessary.

5 Pour the infused ganache into the prepared baking mat and leave to set overnight in a cool, dry area. Brush the surface with chocolate cocoa butter solution and then continue with steps 4–7 of how to make an infused or flavoured ganache chocolate on page 45.

6 Decorate by sprinkling with dried rosemary strips and leave to fully set for about 2 hours in a cool, dry area.

Herb Variations

Richmond Park Honey

Follow the recipe above but replace the rosemary with 60g (2oz) Richmond Park honey and omit the invert sugar, olive oil and salt. Boil the honey with the cream (there is no need to leave to infuse or pass through a sieve (strainer)). Use 400g (14oz) fine dark (bittersweet) chocolate (63% cocoa solids) mixed with 130g (4½oz) fine milk chocolate.

Jasmine

Follow the recipe above using these ingredients: 350ml (12fl oz/scant 1½ cups) whipping (pouring) cream; 6g (1 tsp) fresh jasmine flowers; 60g (2oz) invert sugar; 260g (9¼oz) fine milk chocolate; 400g (14oz) fine dark (bittersweet) chocolate (63% cocoa solids); and 60g (2oz) unsalted butter. Leave the cream to infuse for 4 hours instead of 2 and press a piece of acetate onto the corner of the chocolate to decorate.

Fresh Lavender

Follow the recipe above but replace the rosemary with 5g (½ tsp) fresh lavender, and use 60g (2oz) of both invert sugar and unsalted butter. Omit the olive oil and salt. Also use a mix of 130g (4½oz) fine milk chocolate and 375g (13oz) fine dark (bittersweet) chocolate (65% cocoa solids) instead of just dark chocolate. Decorate with dried lavender on top of the chocolate.

Thai Basil

Follow the recipe above but replace the herb with 10g (1/4 oz) Thai basil leaves and omit the oil and salt. Decorate with dried Thai basil strips *(see box)*.

Top to bottom:
Couture Chocolates with Sweet Herbs
Rosemary & Olive Oil;
Richmond Park Honey;
Jasmine;
Fresh Lavender;
and Thai Basil.

COUTURE CHOCOLATES WITH SAVOURY HERBS

Tarragon & Mustard

Be careful not to add any herbs to boiling cream as it can weaken the flavour and destroy the aroma. This chocolate is very eye-catching.

Makes about 80 chocolates

1 quantity **Chocolate Cocoa Butter Solution** *(see page 29)*
1 quantity **Tarragon & Mustard Ganache** *(see pages 48–51)*
500g (1lb 2oz) tempered fine dark (bittersweet) chocolate *(see pages 18–19)*, to coat
Crushed mustard seeds, to decorate

1 Line a baking tray (sheet) with a non-stick baking mat and brush it liberally with the chocolate cocoa butter solution.

2 Make the tarragon and mustard infused ganache as instructed on pages 48–51.

3 Pour the infused ganache into the prepared baking mat and leave to set overnight in a cool, dry area.

4 Brush the surface with some more chocolate cocoa butter solution and then continue with steps 4–7 of how to make an infused or flavoured ganache chocolate on page 45.

5 Decorate by sprinkling with the crushed mustard seeds and leave to fully set for about 2 hours in a cool, dry area.

Savoury Herb Variations

Fresh Mint

Follow the recipe above but replace the tarragon with 40g (1½oz) mint leaves (washed and dried) and omit the mustard powder. Decorate by placing each chocolate on an embossed acetate sheet *(see Directory, page 224)* once dipped to create a pattern on the base of the chocolate.

Thyme & Scottish Heather Honey

Follow the recipe above but replace the tarragon with 2.5g (½ tsp) lemon thyme leaves (washed and dried), omit the mustard powder and replace the invert sugar with 60g (2oz) Scottish heather honey. Use only 350ml (12fl oz/scant 1½ cups) of whipping (pouring) cream and a mixture of 400g (14oz) fine dark (bittersweet) chocolate (66% cocoa solids) and 125g (4½oz) fine milk chocolate. Decorate by placing each chocolate on an embossed acetate sheet *(see Directory, page 224)* once dipped to create a pattern on the base of the chocolate.

Shiso

Follow the recipe above but replace the tarragon with 10g (¼oz) fresh shiso leaves (washed and dried) and omit the mustard powder. Decorate by placing each chocolate on an embossed acetate sheet *(see Directory, page 224)* once dipped to create a pattern on the base of the chocolate.

Top to bottom:
Couture Chocolates with Savoury Herbs
Tarragon & Mustard;
Fresh Mint;
Thyme & Scottish Heather Honey;
and Shiso.

JAPANESE COUTURE CHOCOLATES

Green Tea

Makes about 80 chocolates

1 quantity **Chocolate Cocoa Butter
Solution** (see page 29)
375ml (12fl oz/1½ cups) whipping
(pouring) cream
15g (½oz) green tea leaves
55g (scant 2oz) invert sugar
200g (7oz) fine milk chocolate, chopped
290g (10oz) fine dark (bittersweet)
chocolate (66% cocoa solids), chopped
60g (2oz/5 tbsp) unsalted butter, cut into
cubes and at room temperature
500g (1lb 2oz) tempered fine dark
(bittersweet) chocolate (see pages 18–19)
Sen cha leaves (Japanese green tea)

1 Line a baking tray (sheet) with a
non-stick baking mat and brush with
the chocolate cocoa butter solution.
Put the cream in a saucepan and bring
to the boil. Take off the heat and
allow to cool slightly before adding the
green tea leaves. Cover with cling film
(plastic wrap) and leave to infuse for
4 hours. Pass the cream through a fine
sieve (strainer) to catch the tea leaves.
Return the cream to the saucepan,
add the invert sugar and bring to
the boil again. Take off the heat and
leave to cool until it reaches 65–70°C
(149–158°F).

2 Melt the chocolate in a bowl over a
bain-marie (water bath) to about 45°C
(113°F) and gradually add the cooled
cream to the chocolate. Continue to
mix to form an emulsion. Add the
butter and continue to mix until fully
incorporated. Blend with a hand-held
blender if necessary. Pour the ganache
into the prepared baking mat and leave
to set overnight in a cool, dry area.

3 Brush the surface with chocolate
cocoa butter and and then continue

with steps 4–7 of how to make an
infused ganache chocolate on page 45.
Decorate with the Sen cha leaves and
leave to fully set in a cool, dry area.

Japanese
Flavour Variations

Houji Cha (smoked green tea)
Follow the Green Tea recipe but
replace the green tea leaves with 12g
(⅓oz) Houji cha tea leaves. Decorate
with ground houji cha leaves.

Japanese Black Vinegar
Follow the Green Tea recipe omitting
the green tea leaves. Just boil 395ml
(13½fl oz/1⅔ cups) cream once with
the invert sugar and then mix into
450g (1lb) fine dark (bittersweet)
chocolate (70% cocoa solids). Also
add 25g (scant 1oz) Japanese black
vinegar when you add the butter.
Decorate by placing each chocolate
on an embossed acetate sheet (see
Directory, page 224).

Yuzu (Japanese citrus fruit)
Follow the Green Tea recipe but
replace the green tea leaves with 7g
(1 tsp) yuzu zest (see page 218).
Replace the mix of fine milk and dark
(bittersweet) chocolate with 450g (1lb)
dark (bittersweet) chocolate (with 66%
cocoa solids). Decorate with dried yuzu
zest (see box, page 68).

Matcha (green tea powder)
Follow the Green Tea recipe but
replace the green tea leaves with 25g
(scant 1oz) matcha powder. Just boil
the cream once with the invert sugar,
mix a small amount with the matcha
powder to make a paste, then return
to the rest of the cream. Continue
as per the recipe and decorate with a
sprinkling of matcha powder.

Apricot & wasabi

Makes about 80 chocolates

½ quantity **Pâté de Fruits** (see pages
56–57 – replace the raspberry purée
and fresh raspberries with 325g (11oz)
apricot purée)

For the wasabi ganache
2.5g (¼–½ tsp) wasabi powder
5ml (1 tsp) water
180ml (6fl oz/¾ cup) whipping
(pouring) cream
25g (scant 1oz) invert sugar (see page 23)
210g (7½oz) fine dark (bittersweet)
chocolate (66% cocoa solids), chopped
30g (1oz/2 tbsp) unsalted butter, cut into
cubes and at room temperature
1 quantity of **Chocolate Cocoa Butter
Solution** (see page 29)
500g (1lb 2oz) tempered fine dark
(bittersweet) chocolate (see pages 18–19)

1 Mix together the wasabi powder and
water to make a paste. Line a baking
tray (sheet) with a non-stick baking
mat. Put the cream and invert sugar in
a saucepan and bring to the boil. Take
off the heat and leave to cool until it
reaches 65–70°C (149–158°F). Blend
a small amount of the cream with the
wasabi paste and mix to a loose paste.
Add it back to the cream and mix well.

2 Melt the chocolate over a bain-marie
(water bath) to about 45°C (113°F) and
add the cooled cream to the chocolate.
Continue to mix to form an emulsion.
Add the butter and continue to mix until
fully incorporated. Blend with a hand
blender if necessary.

3 Make a jelly layered chocolate with
the flavoured pâté de fruits and ganache
following the instructions on page 47.
Decorate by placing each chocolate on
an embossed acetate sheet.

Clockwise from top:

Japanese Couture Chocolates
Houji Cha (smoked Tea);
Green tea;
Matcha (green tea powder);
Apricot & Wasabi;
Japanese Black Vinegar;
and Yuzu (Japanese citrus fruit).

FRUITY COUTURE CHOCOLATES

Raspberry & Toscano

The fruity notes in the chocolate work tremendously well with the raspberry. We also tend to leave the seed in the pâté de fruits, thus adding a little texture.

Makes about 80 chocolates

½ quantity Raspberry **Pâté de Fruits**
  (see pages 56–57)
145ml (4½fl oz/generous ½ cup)
  whipping (pouring) cream
30g (1oz) invert sugar (see page 23)
165g (5½oz) fine dark (bittersweet)
  chocolate (63% cocoa solids),
  finely chopped
30g (1oz/2 tbsp) unsalted butter, cut into
  cubes and at room temperature
1 quantity **Chocolate Cocoa Butter
  Solution** (see page 29)
500g (1lb 2oz) tempered fine dark
  (bittersweet) chocolate
  (see pages 18–19), to coat

1 Pour the raspberry pâté de fruits into a baking tray (sheet) lined with a non-stick baking mat and leave to set overnight in a cool, dry area.

2 Put the cream and invert sugar in a saucepan and bring to the boil. Take off the heat and leave to cool until it reaches 65–70°C (149–158°F).

3 Melt the chocolate in a bowl over a bain-marie (water bath) to about 45°C (113°F) and gradually add the cooled cream to the chocolate. Continue to mix to form an emulsion. Add the butter and continue to mix until fully incorporated. Blend with a hand blender if necessary.

4 Pour the ganache on top of the pâté de fruits and leave to set overnight in a cool, dry area.

5 Brush the surface with some chocolate cocoa butter solution and then continue with steps 5–8 of how to make a jelly-layered chocolate on page 47. Decorate by placing each chocolate on an embossed acetate sheet (see Directory, page 224) to create a pattern on the base of the chocolate. Leave to fully set in a cool, dry area.

Flavour Variations

Apple & Bramble
Follow the Raspberry & Toscano recipe but make the pâté de fruits with 325g (11oz) apple purée and 5ml (1 tsp) lemon juice and the ganache with 125g (4½oz) ready-made bramble purée (OR see Blackcurrant Purée, page 124) instead of the cream.

Juniper Berry & Blackcurrant
Follow the Raspberry & Toscano recipe but make the pâté de fruits with 275g (9½oz) Blackcurrant Purée (see page 124) and 50g (1¾oz) fresh blackcurrants. Bring the cream to the boil, add 5g (¾ tsp) juniper berries, cover with cling film (plastic wrap) and leave to infuse for 4 hours before straining through a fine sieve (strainer). Then continue from step 2. Decorate with cassis powder.

Passion Fruit & Mango
A great summer chocolate – perfect with a glass of fizz.

Makes about 80 chocolates

1 quantity **Chocolate Cocoa Butter
  Solution** (see page 29)
125g (4½oz) passion fruit purée
125g (4½oz) mango purée (see page 23)
35g (1¼oz) caster (surperfine) sugar
75ml (2½fl oz/scant ⅓ cup) whipping
  (pouring) cream
60g (2oz) invert sugar (see page 23)
300g (10oz) fine dark (bittersweet)
  chocolate (63% cocoa solids), chopped
180g (6½oz) fine milk chocolate
  (32% cocoa solids), finely chopped
60g (2oz/5 tbsp) unsalted butter, cut into
  cubes and at room temperature
500g (1lb 2oz) tempered fine dark
  (bittersweet) chocolate (see pages 18–19)

1 Line a baking tray (sheet) with a non-stick baking mat and brush it liberally with the chocolate cocoa butter solution. Put both fruit purées, the caster (superfine) sugar, whipping (pouring) cream and invert sugar in a saucepan and bring to the boil. Take off the heat and leave to cool until it reaches 65–70°C (149–158°F).

2 Melt the chocolate over a bain-marie (water bath) to about 45°C (113°F) and gradually add the cooled fruit cream to the chocolate. Continue to mix to form an emulsion. Add the butter and continue to mix until fully incorporated. Blend with a hand blender if necessary. Pour into the prepared mat and leave to set overnight in a cool, dry area.

3 Brush the surface with chocolate cocoa butter solution and then continue with steps 4–7 of how to make an infused or flavoured ganache chocolate on page 45. Decorate by placing on an embossed acetate sheet to create a pattern on the base of the chocolate. Leave to set in a cool, dry area.

Top to bottom:

Fruity Couture Chocolates
Apple & Bramble;
Raspberry & Toscano;
Passion Fruit & Mango;
and Juniper Berry & Blackcurrant.

MAKING CHOCOLATES IN MOULDS

We use this method for making our soft caramel chocolates as they need to be protected by a shell, although you can use alternative fillings (a flavoured or infused ganache, the Chocolate Coconut Bar filling *(see page 114)* or the Feuillantine Base *(see pages 54–55)* for example). You can buy pre-made shells, but the quality of the chocolate tends to be poor, so I find it much more fun and satisfying to make my own. See the Directory on page 224 for where to buy chocolate moulds.

> **Note:** Always use tempered chocolate *(see pages 18–19)* when filling moulds.

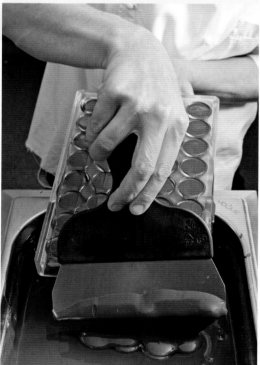

1 Fill the chocolate mould with tempered chocolate.

2 Scrape off the excess chocolate with a scraper and also use the scraper to tap the sides of the mould to remove any air bubbles.

3 Turn the mould upside down over a bowl and tap with the scraper again – the majority of the chocolate should fall out into the bowl underneath to leave a shell of chocolate coating each hole. Turn the right way up and scrape off the excess chocolate with the scraper. Place the mould upside down on a baking tray (sheet) lined with silicone (baking) paper. Leave it to set for 10–15 minutes in a cool, dry area.

4 Spoon the cooled caramel (or other filling) into a piping (pastry) bag and snip a small hole in the end of the bag – not too big or the caramel will flow too fast. Pipe the caramel into the moulds filling them until they are ⅘ full.

5 Pour more tempered chocolate over the top of the mould so that each hole is completely filled and level off with a palette knife. Leave the mould to fully set for at least 2–3 hours in a cool, dry area.

6 Once set, twist the mould to loosen the chocolates, turn it upside down and tap gently so that the chocolates drop out of the mould.

COUTURE CARAMEL CHOCOLATES

Caramels are a big favourite in our shops, salted being the most popular. This year our Muscovado Caramel was voted the best overall chocolate at the Academy of Chocolate Awards. Our diverse range should cover all tastes, but through trial and error you may come up with your own classic.

Don't be daunted by making caramel, it is simpler than you think. I like our caramel to have a deep, rich flavour you can only achieve by cooking the sugar to an amber caramel — you will know if you have achieved this by a haze coming from the caramel. Always have your boiled cream to hand to stop the cooking. We use the finest French butter with fleur de sel — choose your butter carefully as it will determine the quality of your caramel.

Sea Salt Caramel

A well-cooked caramel with the addition of salt balances the sweetness, allowing that wonderfully rich, natural caramel flavour to shine through.

Note:
All caramel recipes use a 24- or 40-hole chocolate mould (with each hole being at least 1.5cm (½ inch) deep).

Makes about 80 chocolates

185ml (6½fl oz/¾ cup) whipping (pouring) cream
1 vanilla pod (bean), split lengthways
375g (13oz/1⅔ cups) caster (superfine) sugar
60g (2oz) liquid glucose

300g (10oz/3 sticks) sea salt butter, cut into cubes and at room temperature
500g (1lb 2oz) tempered fine dark (bittersweet) chocolate
(see pages 18–19)

4

5

6

1 Put the cream in a saucepan. Scrape the seeds from the split vanilla pod (bean) into the cream and drop in the empty pod. Bring to the boil. Take off the heat immediately.

2 Meanwhile, heat an empty heavy-based saucepan. When it is hot, add one-third of the sugar with the liquid glucose and heat slowly until it forms a light caramel and the sugar crystals have dissolved.

3 Add the remaining sugar and continue to cook until you get an amber caramel. This will take about 15 minutes, but there are lots of variables so you must be vigilant and keep watch while it is cooking.

4 Gradually add the warm cream to the caramel. Mix well and then take off the heat.

5 Add the butter, cube by cube. Mix well until it has been fully incorporated and then leave to cool.

6 Fill the moulds with the tempered chocolate and caramel following the instructions on pages 76–77.

Orange & Balsamic Caramel

The idea behind this chocolate was from an orange and caramel sauce I made back in my training days. The acidity from the orange and the balsamic vinegar cuts the richness of the caramel extremely well.

Makes about 80 chocolates

250ml (9fl oz/1 cup) orange juice
¼ vanilla pod (bean), split lengthways
90ml (3fl oz/⅓ cup) whipping
   (pouring) cream
300g (10oz/1⅓ cups) caster
   (superfine) sugar

40g (1½oz) liquid glucose
100g (3½oz/1 stick) unsalted butter, cut
   into cubes and at room temperature
100g (3½oz/1 stick) sea salt butter, cut
   into cubes and at room temperature

12.5ml (2½ tsp) balsamic vinegar
500g (1lb 2oz) tempered fine dark
   (bittersweet) chocolate
   (see pages 18–19)

1

1 (reduced juice)

3

1 Put the orange juice in a saucepan. Scrape the seeds from the split vanilla pod (bean) into the orange juice and drop in the empty pod. Bring to the boil and continue to cook until it has reduced to about 150ml (5fl oz/⅔ cup), about 8–10 minutes.

2 Put the cream in a saucepan and bring to the boil.

3 Meanwhile, heat an empty heavy-based saucepan. When it is hot, add one-third of the sugar with the liquid glucose and heat slowly until it forms a light caramel and the sugar crystals have dissolved. Add the remaining sugar and continue to cook until you get an amber caramel. This will take about 15 minutes, but there are lots of variables so you must be vigilant and keep watch while it is cooking.

4 Gradually add the warm cream to the caramel. Mix well and then pour in the reduced orange and vanilla juice. Take off the heat.

5 Add both butters, cube by cube, mix well until and then leave to cool. Pour in the vinegar and stir until completely smooth. Fill the mould with the tempered chocolate and caramel following the instructions on pages 76–77.

4

5

SURFACE REMAINS HOT AFTER USE DO NOT TOUCH

SURFACE REMAINS HOT AFTER USE DO NOT TOUCH

COUTURE CARAMEL CHOCOLATES

Ginger Caramel

This chocolate's spicy notes help balance the caramel for a well-rounded finish.

Makes about 80 chocolates

150ml (5fl oz/⅔ cup) whipping (pouring) cream
12g (⅓oz) fresh root ginger, grated
250g (9oz/generous 1 cup) caster (superfine) sugar
40g (1½oz) liquid glucose
60g (2oz) fine dark (bittersweet) chocolate (70% cocoa solids), chopped
90g (3oz/7 tbsp) unsalted butter, cut into cubes and at room temperature
90g (3oz/7 tbsp) sea salt butter, cut into cubes and at room temperature
500g (1lb 2oz) tempered fine dark (bittersweet) chocolate (see pages 18–19), to coat

1 Put the cream and ginger in a saucepan and bring to the boil. Take off the heat and cover with cling film (plastic wrap). Leave to infuse for 30 minutes. Pass through a sieve (strainer).

2 Meanwhile, heat an empty heavy-based saucepan. When it is hot, add one-third of the sugar with the liquid glucose and heat slowly until it forms a light caramel and the sugar crystals have dissolved. Add the remaining sugar and continue to cook until you get an amber caramel. This will take about 15 minutes, but there are lots of variables so you must be vigilant and keep watch while it is cooking.

3 Gradually add the warm cream to the caramel, mixing well and then the chocolate. Add both butters, mix well until it has been fully incorporated and then leave to cool. Fill the moulds with the tempered chocolate and caramel following the instructions on pages 76–77.

Black Olive & Tomato Caramel

Makes about 80 chocolates

125ml (4fl oz/½ cup) whipping (pouring) cream
10g (¼oz) Kalamata black olives, pitted and finely chopped
3 tomatoes, roughly chopped
A pinch of salt and black pepper
1g (¼ tsp) balsamic vinegar
250g (9oz/generous 1 cup) caster (superfine) sugar
40g (1½oz) liquid glucose
200g (7oz/2 sticks) unsalted butter, cut into cubes and at room temperature
500g (1lb 2oz) tempered fine dark (bittersweet) chocolate (see pages 18–19), to coat

1 Put the cream and chopped olives in a saucepan and bring to the boil. Take off the heat. Meanwhile, cook the tomato in a saucepan over a low heat for 15 minutes until the moisture has evaporated. Add the salt, pepper and balsamic vinegar. Pass the tomato mixture through a fine sieve (strainer) to make a tomato paste and then leave to cool.

2 Heat an empty heavy-based saucepan. When it is hot, add one-third of the sugar with the liquid glucose and heat slowly until it forms a light caramel and the sugar crystals dissolve. Add the remaining sugar and continue to cook until you get an amber caramel. This will take about 15 minutes.

3 Gradually add the warm cream to the caramel, mixing well. Add the butter, cube by cube. Mix well, leave to cool, then stir in the tomato paste. Leave to cool completely. Fill the moulds with the tempered chocolate and caramel following the instructions on pages 76–77.

Salted Butter & Muscovado Caramel

This was the highest marked chocolate in the Academy of Chocolate Awards 2011.

Makes about 80 chocolates

125ml (4fl oz/½ cup) whipping (pouring) cream
¼ vanilla pod (bean), split lengthways
85g (3oz/generous ⅓ cup) caster (superfine) sugar
40g (1½oz) liquid glucose
85g (3oz/generous ⅓ cup) golden caster (superfine) sugar
200g (7oz/2 sticks) sea salt butter, cut into cubes and at room temperature
125g (4½oz) muscovado sugar
500g (1lb 2oz) tempered fine dark (bittersweet) chocolate (see pages 18–19)

1 Put the cream in a saucepan. Scrape the vanilla seeds from the split vanilla pod (bean) into the cream and drop in the empty pod. Bring to the boil, then take off the heat.

2 Meanwhile, heat an empty heavy-based saucepan. When it is hot, add half of the caster (superfine) sugar with the liquid glucose and heat slowly until it forms a light caramel and the sugar crystals have dissolved. Add the remaining caster sugar and golden caster sugar and continue to cook until you get an amber caramel. This will take about 15 minutes, but there are lots of variables so you must be vigilant. Stir in the muscovado sugar and leave to melt gently over a low heat until it is completely amalgamated.

3 Add the cream to the caramel. Mix and take off the heat. Add the butter. Mix well until it had been fully incorporated and leave to cool. Fill the moulds with the tempered chocolate and caramel following the instructions on pages 76–77.

Note: All caramel recipes use a 24- or 40-hole chocolate mould (with each hole being at least 1.5cm (½ inch) deep).

Top to bottom:
Couture Caramel Chocolates
Ginger Caramel;
Salted Butter & Muscovado Caramel;
Sea Salt Caramel *(see page 79)*;
Orange & Balsamic Caramel *(see page 80)*;
and Black Olive & Tomato Caramel.

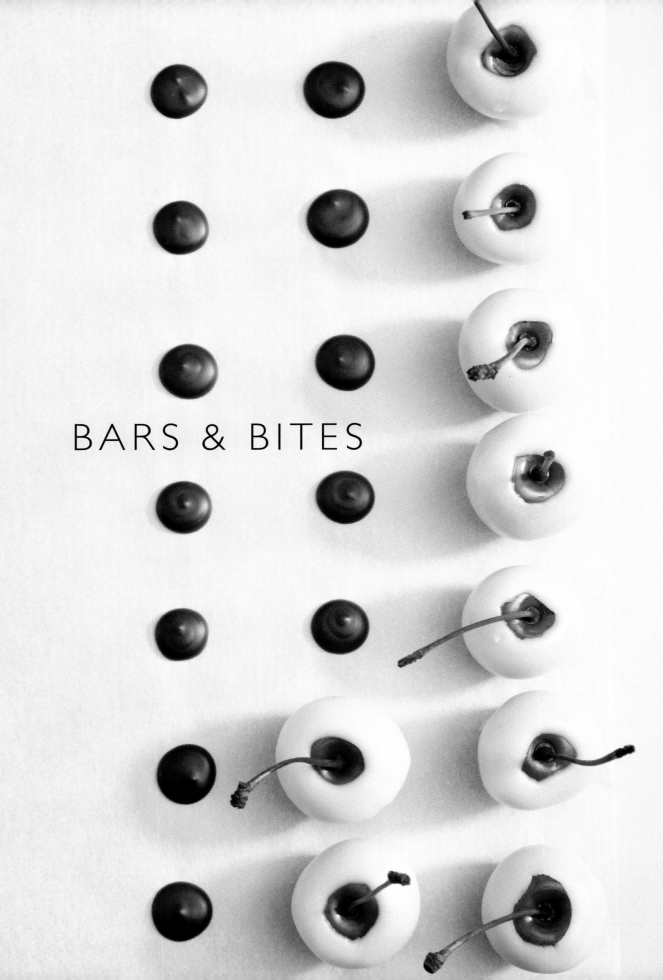

BARS & BITES

BAR DECORATION: Confit Orange

These sweet orange bites are to be used as decoration for your chocolate bars (see page 88). You can also dip these confit strips in tempered chocolate as with the Confit Grapefruit (see page 105) and enjoy on its own.

Makes about 12 pieces

3 navel oranges
500ml (16fl oz/2 cups) water
375g (13oz/1⅔ cups) caster
  (superfine) sugar
1 vanilla pod (bean), split lengthways

1 Score around the outside of the orange into quarters, then gently take off each quarter of the peel. Place the peel into a saucepan and fill with enough water to just cover the peel. Bring to the boil, then drain the peel and discard the water. Refresh the orange peel under cold water. Repeat this process twice more.

2 Place the drained orange peel, water and sugar into a saucepan. Scrape the seeds from the split vanilla pod (bean) into the saucepan and drop in the empty pod, too. Bring to the boil. Reduce the heat to low and continue to cook for a further 30 minutes. Remove the saucepan from the heat and leave it to cool for 30 minutes. Cover with a lid and leave to cool completely overnight.

3 Return the saucepan to the hob and bring to the boil. Reduce the heat to low and cook for a further 2 hours, until the orange is soft and candied. Leave to cool overnight.

4 Drain off any excess syrup (the syrup can be saved and re-used) and place the orange confit onto a wire rack. Leave to dry for 3–4 hours and then cut into thin strips as needed.

BAR DECORATION: Crystallized Salted Pistachios

More decorations for your chocolate bars (see page 88). I would ideally use Sicilian pistachios for this recipe – they are harder to get hold of and more expensive than the average variety, but the quality is well worth it in this case.

Makes about 150g (5½oz/1 cup)

125g (4½oz/¾ cup) pistachios
60g (2oz/scant ⅓ cup) granulated
 (white) sugar

15ml (3 tsp) kirsch
3g (½ tsp) sea salt

1 Preheat the oven to 200°C (400°F/Gas 6). Spread the pistachios out on a non-stick baking tray (sheet) and bake in the preheated oven for 5 minutes, turning halfway through the cooking time. Leave to cool.

2 Put the nuts in a bowl along with the sugar, kirsch and sea salt. Mix together and spoon onto a baking tray (sheet) lined with a non-stick baking mat. Spread out evenly.

3 Bake in the oven for a further 10–12 minutes, turning twice during the cooking time to ensure an even roast. Leave to cool, then use immediately or store in an airtight container until needed.

FRUIT & NUT DECORATED BARS

I love the combination of fruit and nut. These bars are fabulous to look at and are always a talking point in the shop. Feel free to create your own versions.

Confit Orange
Makes 6 bars

850g (1lb 14oz) tempered fine dark (bittersweet) chocolate *(see pages 18–19)*

85g (3oz) **Confit Orange** *(see page 86)*, cut into strips

60g (2oz/scant ½ cup) roasted hazelnuts, half chopped and half left whole

85g (3oz/scant ½ cup) roasted almonds

40g (1½oz) **Crystallized Salted Pistachios** *(see page 87)*

Apricot & Cranberry
Makes 6 bars

850g (1lb 14oz) tempered fine dark (bittersweet) chocolate *(see pages 18–19)*

150g (5½oz/¾ cup) dried apricots, cut in half

30g (1oz) dried cranberries

60g (2oz) **Crystallized Almonds** (follow the recipe on page 102 but don't dip the almonds in the gianduja)

Autumn Fruits
Makes 6 bars

850g (1lb 14oz) tempered fine dark (bittersweet) chocolate *(see pages 18–19)*

140g (5oz/1 cup) dried pear, cut into slices

30g (1oz) dried apple, cut into slices

10g (¼oz) freeze-dried blackcurrants *(see page 224)*

1 Clean and polish the bar moulds. Pour the tempered chocolate into the cavities and tap on a hard surface to eliminate any air pockets.

2 Use a scraper to scrape along the top of the moulds to produce a flat surface.

Note: You will need two 3-hole 8 × 16cm (3¼ × 6½ inch) bar moulds *(see page 224)*.

3 Gently push in the toppings, evenly spacing them around the chocolate. Leave the bar moulds to set, uncovered, for at least 3–4 hours in a cool, dry area, uncovered.

4 Gently tap out the bars onto a clean flat surface.

3

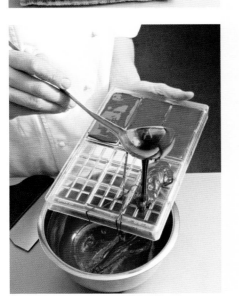

4

5

INFUSED BARS
We have developed our recipes using only natural ingredients – it takes a bit longer, but the results are worth it.

Rosemary & Sea Salt
Makes 9 bars

5.5g (1 tsp) rosemary, washed and dried
500g (1lb 2 oz) tempered fine dark
  (bittersweet) chocolate
  (see pages 18–19)
1g (a pinch) sea salt

For the herb infusion
5.5g (1 tsp) rosemary, washed and dried
25g (scant 1oz) cocoa butter

1 Clean and polish the bar moulds. Finely slice half of the rosemary and place on a baking tray (sheet). Preheat the oven to the lowest setting, about 110°C (200°F/Gas ¼), leave the oven door ajar and dry the rosemary in the oven for 1 hour or until the leaves have dried. Set aside until needed.

2 To make the herb infusion, heat the cocoa butter in a saucepan until it reaches 60°C (140°F) on a sugar thermometer and add the rosemary. Cover with a lid and leave the saucepan in a warm area to infuse overnight.

3 Reheat the cocoa butter mixture, let it cool slightly, then pass it through a fine sieve (strainer).

4 Mix half of the infused cocoa butter solution into the tempered chocolate (the remaining herb infusion can be stored in an airtight container in a cool dry area for use another time).

5 Pour into 9 holes on the bar moulds.

6 Decorate the chocolate with the dried rosemary and sea salt and leave it to set, uncovered, for at least 3–4 hours in a cool, dry area. Gently tap out the bars onto a clean, flat surface.

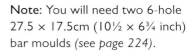

Note: You will need two 6-hole 27.5 × 17.5cm (10½ × 6¾ inch) bar moulds *(see page 224)*.

Variations:
Choose from these further two combinations or use your favourite flavours to make up your own.

Basil & Black Pepper
Makes 9 bars

6g (1 tsp) basil (half should be dried and
  half added to the cocoa butter)
25g (scant 1oz) cocoa butter
500g (1lb 2oz) tempered fine dark
  (bittersweet) chocolate *(see pages 18–19)*
1.5g (¼ tsp) freshly ground black pepper

Mint
Makes 9 bars

8g (1¼ tsp) mint (3g/½ tsp should be
  dried; the rest added to the cocoa butter)
25g (scant 1oz) cocoa butter
500g (1lb 2oz) tempered fine dark
  (bittersweet) chocolate *(see pages 18–19)*

6

FEUILLANTINE BAR

This is one of my favourite bars, bursting with our homemade praline and Piedmont hazelnuts.

Note: You will need one curved 8-hole 27.5 × 13.5cm (10½ × 5¼ inch) bar mould (*see page 224*).

Makes 8 bars

20g (¾oz) Piedmont hazelnuts, roughly chopped
65g (2¼oz) feuillantine wafers (*see page 218 and 224*)
75g (2½oz) fine milk chocolate (32% cocoa solids), finely chopped
50g (1¾oz) **Praline Paste** (*see pages 158–159*)
500g (1lb 2oz) tempered fine dark (bittersweet) chocolate (*see pages 18–19*)

3

6

7

1 Clean and polish the bar moulds.

2 Mix together the chopped hazelnuts with the feuillantine wafers in a small bowl and set aside.

3 Melt the milk chocolate in a bowl over a bain-marie (water bath) to 45°C (113°F). Mix in the praline paste and take off the heat. Mix in the feuillantine wafers and hazelnuts.

4 Pour the tempered chocolate into the bar moulds and tap on a hard surface to eliminate any air pockets.

5 Tip up the bar moulds to pour the chocolate back into the bowl and scrape along the surface to obtain a chocolate casing for the praline filling. Leave the bar moulds to set, uncovered, for about 20 minutes in a cool, dry area.

6 Spoon the praline mixture into the moulds until it has almost filled the cavity, then level with a palette knife.

7 Pour the remaining tempered chocolate over the top of the feuilletine filling and scrape along the surface to seal the top.

8 Leave the moulds to set, uncovered, for at least 2–3 hours in a cool, dry area until the chocolate has come away from the mould.

9 Gently tap out the bars onto a clean, flat surface.

WALNUT BRITTLE

This has been one of our most recent creations – the buttery notes of the walnuts coated with a caramelized nougatine balanced against the dark chocolate.

Makes about 12 shards

40g (1½oz/3 tbsp) unsalted butter
80g (2¾oz/generous ⅓ cup) caster (superfine) sugar
30g (1oz) liquid glucose
100g (3½oz/1 cup) walnuts, roughly chopped
500g (1lb 2oz) tempered fine dark (bittersweet) chocolate *(see pages 18–19)*

3

3

4

1 Preheat the oven to 200°C (400°F/Gas 6) and line a baking tray (sheet) with a non-stick baking mat.

2 Melt the butter, sugar and glucose in a saucepan over a medium heat. Remove from the heat and mix in the chopped walnuts.

3 Spread the walnut mixture out onto the baking mat and bake in the preheated oven for 8–10 minutes until the mixture is caramelized. Remove from the oven and leave to cool.

4 Roughly break the walnut brittle into shards.

5 Dip the walnut shards in the tempered chocolate so that they are completely coated and place them on a baking tray (sheet) lined with silicone (baking) paper to set.

6 Leave to set for at least 1 hour in a cool, dry area.

CHOCOLATE THINS

Toasted Sesame Seeds & Milk Chocolate

I like to use milk chocolate that has caramel notes and I always toast the sesame seeds to release the flavour.

Makes 2 large sheets that will break into about 30 thins

50g (1¾oz) white sesame seeds
50g (1¾oz) dark sesame seeds
500g (1lb 2oz) tempered fine milk
chocolate *(see pages 18–19)*

1

1 In a frying pan (skillet), lightly toast the white and dark sesame seeds over moderate heat for a few minutes. Stir the white and dark sesame seeds into the tempered chocolate until they are evenly mixed.

2 Spread a thin layer of the chocolate onto an acetate sheet or a sheet of silicone (baking) paper.

3 Place another piece of acetate or silicone (baking) paper on top and place between two flat baking trays (sheets) or perspex sheets. Repeat this process to make a second sheet. Leave to set for at least 2 hours in a cool, dry area.

2

4 Remove the top tray or sheet and carefully remove the top acetate sheet or silicone (baking) paper and break into pieces or shards.

> **Note:** You will need 4 acetate sheets measuring about 30 × 40cm (12 × 16 inch) or silicone (baking) paper (your thins will not be as shiny if not using acetate sheets).

3

White Chocolate & Cocoa Nibs

We rarely use white chocolate as it lacks cocoa intensity – here the thins are topped with cocoa nibs to get that cocoa hit.

Makes 2 large sheets that will break into about 30 thins

10g (¾oz) runny honey
30g (1½oz) cocoa nibs
500g (1lb 2oz) tempered fine white
chocolate *(see pages 18–19)*

1 Preheat the oven to it's lowest setting (probably about 100°C/212°F/Gas ¼) and line a baking tray (sheet) with a non-stick baking mat.

2 In a saucepan, warm the honey over a moderate heat and mix in the cocoa nibs.

3 Spread the cocoa nibs out on the baking mat and transfer them to the oven for about 2 hours – leave the oven door slightly ajar to keep the temperature as low as possible. Leave to cool, then either use immediately or store in an airtight container.

4 Spread a thin layer of the tempered white chocolate onto an acetate sheet or a sheet of silicone (baking) paper and sprinkle with the honey-coated cocoa nibs. Place another piece of acetate or silicone (baking) paper on top and place between two flat baking trays (sheets) or perspex sheets. Repeat this process to make a second sheet. Leave to set for at least 2 hours in a cool, dry area.

6 Remove the top tray (sheet) and carefully remove the top acetate sheet or silicone (baking) paper and break into pieces or shards.

CHOCOLATE LOLLIPOPS

These are great fun to make – an ideal way to get your children into the kitchen and working with chocolate.

Flavour combinations Each makes 15 lollipops

Fine dark chocolate with crystallized pistachio, toasted sesame & cranberries

200g (7oz) tempered fine dark (bittersweet) chocolate *(see pages 18–19)*
3g (½ tsp) lightly toasted white sesame seeds
16g (½oz) **Crystallized Salted Pistachios** *(see page 87)*
20g (¾oz) dried cranberries

Fine milk chocolate with confit orange, crystallized pistachio & cocoa nibs

200g (7oz) tempered fine milk chocolate *(see pages 18–19)*
16g (½oz) **Crystallized Salted Pistachios** *(see page 87)*
15g (½oz) **Confit Orange** *(see page 86),* cut into 3cm (1 inch) strips
3g (½ tsp) cocoa nibs

Fine white chocolate with almond batons, freeze-dried raspberries & black sesame seeds

200g (7oz) tempered fine white chocolate *(see pages 18–19)*
3g (½ tsp) lightly toasted black sesame seeds
12g (⅓oz) roasted almond batons
3g (½ tsp) freeze-dried raspberries *(see page 224)*

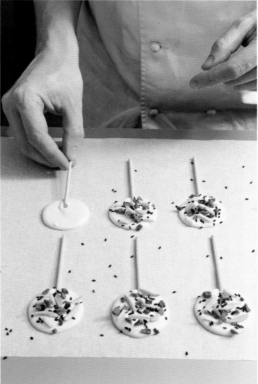

1 Use a pencil to draw fifteen 4.5cm (1¾ inch) diameter circles on some silicone (baking) paper. With a teaspoon, fill in each circle with the tempered chocolate.

2 Place lolly sticks into the chocolate discs and make sure they are well covered so that they will be secure.

3 Decorate each disc of chocolate with your chosen toppings. Leave to set for 2–3 hours in a cool, dry area.

FLORENTINES

An Italian biscuit made of caramelized fruits and nuts. There are many variations; we keep ours simple with almonds, confit orange and chocolate.

Makes 20

20 chocolate discs (follow the Flat Sheet
   Techniques on page 157 and use a 6cm
   (2½ inch) round cutter)

25g (scant 1oz/2 tbsp) unsalted butter

75g (2½oz/⅓ cup) caster
   (superfine) sugar

10g (¼oz/½ tbsp) plain
   (all-purpose) flour

65ml (2fl oz/¼ cup) whipping
   (pouring) cream

50g (1¾oz/½ cup) flaked almonds

50g (1¾oz/¼ cup) baton almonds
   (or whole blanched almonds,
   roughly chopped)

75g (2½oz) **Confit Orange**
   (see page 86), chopped

500g (1lb 2oz) tempered fine dark
   (bittersweet) chocolate
   (see pages 18–19)

Note: You will need a 6cm
(2½ inch) round cutter and
two 12-cup silicone bun trays
(see page 224).

---

1 Make 20 chocolate discs from the tempered dark chocolate following the instructions in Flat Sheet Techniques on page 157. Use a 6cm (2½ inch) round cutter to cut discs instead of squares.

2 Preheat the oven to 200°C (400°F/Gas 6).

3 In a saucepan, melt the butter over moderate heat. Take off the heat and mix in the sugar and flour. Slowly incorporate the cream and mix until smooth. Add the flaked and baton almonds and the confit orange.

4 Spoon 1 tablespoon of the mixture into 20 of the cups on the silicone bun trays. Bake in the oven for 10–12 minutes until golden brown and caramelized. Leave to cool slightly, then remove from the trays. Place on wire racks and leave to cool completely.

5 Spread the tempered chocolate over the smooth side of the baked florentines.

6 Top each florentine with a chocolate disc then spread with tempered chocolate again. Using a comb scraper, run across the chocolate to create a wave effect.

7 Leave to set for at least 1 hour in a cool, dry area.

1

5

6

FOUR BITES

Bars & Bites are a mixture of classic and contemporary. We try to introduce some interesting combinations to our craft, while using classic techniques.

Crystallized Almonds in Gianduja

Here, we have crystallized the almonds to add crunch and then rolled in the most fabulous gianduja to add another dimension to the normal roasted nuts.

Makes about 12 portions

400g (14oz/2 cups) whole almonds
(preferably Avola)
125g (4½oz/generous ½ cup)
caster (superfine) sugar
25ml (scant 1fl oz/1½ tbsp) water
250g (9oz/2½ cups) cocoa powder
400g (14oz) gianduja
(see pages 218–219)

6

1 Preheat the oven to 200°C (400°F/ Gas 6). Spread the almonds out on a non-stick baking tray (sheet) and lightly roast for 5–6 minutes in the preheated oven. Place them in a heavy-based pan.

2 In a separate saucepan, cook the sugar and water over a medium heat until it reaches about 118°C (244°F). Pour this sugar syrup over the roasted almonds in the heavy-based pan.

3 Cook the almonds over a moderate heat, stirring continuously, until a frosty white coating forms around the almonds and the sugar crystallizes – this should take about 5–6 minutes.

4 Remove the pan from the heat and spread the crystallized almonds onto a non-stick baking mat. Separate out all of the almonds so that they are evenly dispersed. Leave to cool and harden.

5 Put the cocoa powder in a shallow dish or tray. Melt the gianduja in a bowl over a bain-marie (water bath) to 45°C (113°F) and then cool to 31–32°C (88–90°F).

6 Carefully drop the almonds into the melted gianduja a few at a time. Lift out with a dipping fork, drop into the cocoa powder and roll to fully coat. Repeat with the remaining almonds.

7 Leave to set for 10 minutes and then sieve or shake off the excess cocoa powder.

8 Store in an airtight container until needed.

Suisse Rochers

These nutty clusters date back hundreds of years and are always a staple in artisan chocolate shops.

Makes about 12 portions

400g (14oz/4 cups) almond batons
160g (5½oz/generous ⅔ cup) caster
(superfine) sugar
45ml (1½fl oz/2 tbsp) water
20g (¾oz/1¾ tbsp) unsalted butter
500g (1lb 2oz) tempered fine dark
(bittersweet) or milk chocolate
(see pages 18–19)

1 Preheat the oven to 180°C (350°F/Gas 4) and line 1–2 baking trays (sheets) with non-stick baking mats. Spread the almonds out on the baking mats and lightly roast in the preheated oven for 10 minutes. Remove from the oven and transfer to a heavy-based pan.

2 In a separate saucepan, cook the sugar and water over a medium heat until it reaches about 118°C (244°F). Pour this sugar syrup over the roasted almonds in the heavy-based pan.

3 Cook the almonds over a moderate heat, stirring continuously, until a frosty white coating forms around the almonds and the sugar crystallizes – this should take about 5–6 minutes.

4 Remove the pan from the heat and stir in the butter until it has fully melted. Spread the almonds onto a non-stick baking mat and separate out all of the nuts. Leave to cool and harden.

5 Place half the nuts in a bowl, gradually add half the tempered chocolate, stirring and ensuring the nuts are fully coated. Spoon 3cm (1 inch) clusters onto the lined baking trays (sheets). Repeat with the remaining nuts and chocolate.

1

5

6

3

4

6

Confit Grapefruit with Cocoa Nibs

Although these juicy confit fruits are a little time consuming they are well worth the effort. The cocoa nibs add texture and chocolate intensity and make the bites very moreish – so make sure there are plenty of friends around to share them with.

Makes about 24 pieces

3 pink grapefruits
375g (13oz/1⅔ cups) caster (superfine) sugar
500ml (16fl oz/2 cups) water
1 vanilla pod (bean), split lengthways
500 g (1lb 2oz) tempered fine dark (bittersweet) chocolate (see pages 18–19)
60g (2oz) cocoa nibs

1 Score around the outside of the grapefruit into quarters, gently take off each quarter of the peel and cut in half. Place the peel into a saucepan and fill with enough water to just cover the peel. Bring to the boil, then drain the peel and discard the water. Refresh the peel under cold water. Repeat this process 4 more times.

2 Place the sugar and water in a saucepan. Scrape the seeds from the split vanilla pod (bean) into the pan and drop in the empty pod, too. Bring to the boil. Add the grapefruit peel, reduce the heat to low and continue to cook for a further 30 minutes. Remove the saucepan from the heat and leave it to cool a little. Cover with a lid and leave to cool completely overnight.

3 Return the saucepan to the hob and bring to the boil. Reduce the heat to low and cook for a further 2 hours, until the grapefruit is soft and candied. Leave to cool overnight.

4 Drain off any excess syrup (the syrup can be saved and re-used) and place the grapefruit confit onto a wire rack. Leave to dry for 3–4 hours.

5 Hold a piece of confit grapefruit by its end and dip it into the tempered chocolate so that it is three-quarters coated.

6 Lay it on a non-stick baking mat and sprinkle with cocoa nibs. Repeat with the rest of the confit grapefruit. Leave to set for at least 1 hour in a cool, dry area and then store in an airtight container.

Caramelized Hazelnuts in Kinako Powder

The layers of caramel, chocolate and kinako bring an element of saltiness and enhances the flavour.

Makes about 12 portions

400g (14oz/2⅔ cups) hazelnuts
125g (4½oz/generous ½ cup) caster (superfine) sugar
25ml (scant 1fl oz/1¼ tbsp) water
25g (scant 1oz/2 tbsp) unsalted butter
200g (7oz) tempered fine dark (bittersweet) chocolate (see pages 18–19)
250g (9oz/1⅔ cups) kinako powder (ground roasted soya beans, see page 224)

1 Preheat the oven to 180°C (350°F/ Gas 4). Spread the hazelnuts out on a non-stick baking tray (sheet) and roast in the preheated oven for 10 minutes. Remove from the oven and transfer to a heavy-based pan.

2 In a separate saucepan, cook the sugar and water over a medium heat until it reaches about 118°C (244°F). Pour this sugar syrup over the roasted hazelnuts in the heavy-based pan.

3 Cook the hazelnuts over a moderate heat, stirring continuously, until a frosty white coating forms around the almonds and the sugar crystallizes – this should take about 5–6 minutes.

4 Remove the pan from the heat and stir in the butter until it has fully melted and mixed in. Spread the hazelnuts onto a non-stick baking mat and separate out all of the nuts so that they are evenly dispersed. Leave to cool and harden.

5 Place half the nuts in a bowl, gradually add half the tempered chocolate, stirring and ensuring the nuts are fully coated.

6 Put the kinako powder in a shallow dish or tray and when the chocolate begins to set roll the nuts in the kinako powder until they are fully coated. Repeat with the remaining hazelnuts.

7 Leave to set for 10 minutes and then sieve or shake off the excess kinako powder.

CERISES AU KIRSCH

This is a real classic and really worth the effort – you'll have to be patient as marinating the cherries takes at least 3 months. The best time to eat them is when the fondant starts to break down, normally about 1 week after dipping. Bon appétit.

6

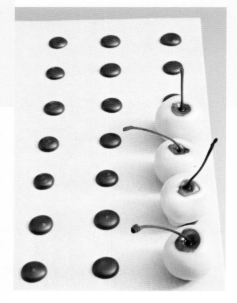

Makes about 30 cherries

300g (10oz) cherries with stalks on
200ml (7fl oz/generous ¾ cup) kirsch
500g (1lb 2oz) tempered fine dark
   (bittersweet) chocolate
   (see pages 18–19)
500g (1¼lb) fondant
1 fine dark chocolate block, for shavings

1 Wash and dry the cherries. Place them in a sterilized Kilner jar and fill with the kirsch. Place small silicone (baking) paper circles on top. Seal the jar and leave to marinate for 3 months.

2 Drain the kirsch from the cherries and reserve it for another use – the kirsch can be used to thin the fondant or in kirsch syrup. Dry the cherries on a cloth or paper towels.

3 Spoon the tempered chocolate into a piping (pastry) bag and pipe small, flat discs onto a non-stick baking mat.

4 In a saucepan, heat the fondant with 20ml (1 tbsp) of the reserved kirsch marinade until it reaches about 55°C (131°F).

5 Hold a cherry by its stalk and dip it into the melted fondant (you will need to regularly stir the fondant to prevent a crust forming).

6 Place onto silicone (baking) paper to set a little and then sit on top of a chocolate disc before it fully sets.

7 Prepare chocolate shavings from the back of a block of chocolate *(see pic above)* and place in a shallow tray.

8 Holding the cherry stalks again, fully dip the fondant-coated cherries into the tempered chocolate. Place each cherry into the chocolate shavings so that the shavings stick to the base of the chocolate-coated cherry.

9 Leave to fully set for at least 1 hour in a cool, dry area.

1

7

5

8

BOUCHÉES

CINDER TOFFEE

This is one of the simplest and most fun confections to make at home. The name 'cinder' comes from the similarity in appearance to a burnt-out piece of coal.

Makes about 20–25 large chunks

50ml (1¾fl oz/3 tbsp) water
190g (6½oz/generous ¾ cup) caster (superfine) sugar
50g (1¾oz/¼ cup) light soft brown sugar
150g (5½oz) liquid glucose
50g (1¾oz) honey
10g (¼oz) bicarbonate of soda (baking soda), sifted
500g (1lb 2oz) tempered dark chocolate (*see pages 18–19*), to coat
500g (1lb 2oz) tempered fine milk chocolate (*see pages 18–19*), to coat

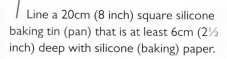

1 Line a 20cm (8 inch) square silicone baking tin (pan) that is at least 6cm (2½ inch) deep with silicone (baking) paper.

2 In a large pan, mix together the water, sugar, brown sugar, glucose and honey. Gently heat until the sugars have dissolved and then increase the temperature and bring to the boil until it reaches 144–146°C (291–295°F). Immediately take the pan off the heat.

3 Add the bicarbonate of soda (baking soda), stirring at the same time. The mix will start to rise to the top of the pan, at which point pour it into the prepared tin (pan). Leave it to cool and set in a cool, dry area.

4 Carefully break the toffee into chunks. Using a dipping fork, coat each piece in tempered chocolate (some in milk and some in dark). It is important to ensure the toffee is fully coated as any uncovered areas will become sticky and soft. Store in an airtight container for up to 1 month.

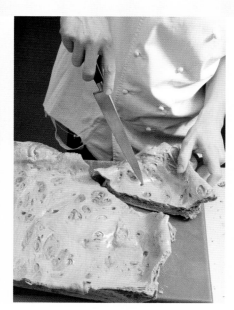

MILLIONAIRE'S SHORTBREAD

This brings back fond memories as my grandmother, who was a great cook, often made cakes and biscuits for family occasions, including these shortbread. It has a Scottish origin – traditionally, it is topped with milk chocolate, but we use fine dark (bittersweet) chocolate to balance the sweet caramel.

Makes about 20 shortbread

½ quantity Sea Salt Caramel
  (see page 79)
500g (1lb 2oz) tempered fine dark
  (bittersweet) chocolate
  (see pages 18–19)
Edible gold leaf, to decorate (optional)

For the shortbread

125g (4½oz/1¼ sticks) unsalted butter,
  cut into cubes and at
  room temperature
185g (6½oz/1¼ cups) plain
  (all-purpose) flour, sifted
60g (2oz/¼ cup) caster
  (superfine) sugar

1 To make the shortbread, put the butter, flour and sugar in the bowl of an electric mixer and combine until the mixture comes together. Remove the dough from the bowl and roll out to 12mm (½ inch) thick on a lightly floured surface. Cut into rectangles measuring 7.5 × 2.5cm (3 × 1 inch) and put into a 20-hole silicone chocolate bar mould (see page 224). Alternatively, you could leave the dough whole and use it to line a 25.5 × 30cm (10 × 12 inch) baking tray (sheet) lined with silicone (baking) paper. Leave to rest for at least 1 hour in the fridge. Preheat the oven to 160°C (325°F/Gas 3) and bake for 20–25 minutes until lightly golden. Leave to cool.

2 Pour 20g (¾oz/1 tbsp) of the sea salt caramel on top of each shortbread base (or pour all of it on top of the layer of shortbread in the baking tray/sheet) and leave to set overnight in a cool, dry area.

3 To make the chocolate sheets, use the tempered chocolate to make 20 rectangles measuring 7.5 × 2.5cm (3 × 1 inch) following the Flat Sheet Technique on page 157.

4 To assemble, remove the shortbread and caramel slices from the mould (or the baking tray (sheet) and then cut into rectangles) and place a sheet of tempered chocolate on top of each slice. Decorate with gold leaf, if using. Store in an airtight container in a cool, dry area and eat within 2–3 days.

CHOCOLATE ROCHERS

Rocher means 'rock' in French, which perfectly describes its shape. They are made with an intense praline and coated in either milk or dark chocolate.

Makes about 16 rochers

100g (3½oz) fine milk chocolate (with
  32% cocoa solids), finely chopped
10g (2 tsp) cocoa butter
75g (2½oz) **Praline Paste**
  (see pages 158–159)
75g (2½oz) feuillantine wafers
75g (2½oz/generous ⅓ cup) roasted
  almonds, cut into strips
500g (1lb 2oz) tempered fine dark
  (bittersweet) chocolate
  (see pages 18–19), to coat
OR
500g (1lb 2oz) tempered fine milk
  chocolate (see pages 18–19), to coat

1 Melt the milk chocolate and cocoa butter over a bain-marie (water bath) until it reaches 45°C (113°F), then mix in the praline paste. Add the feuillantine wafers and almond strips and mix together. Set the bain-marie (water bath) to one side and leave the mixture to cool slightly.

2 Put large spoonfuls of the mix onto silicone (baking) paper and leave to set for about 2 hours in a cool, dry area. Coat the rochers with tempered dark or milk chocolate and leave to set fully. Store in an airtight container in a cool, dry area and eat within 2 weeks.

CHOCOLATE COCONUT BAR

After I enrolled at Glenrothes Technical College this was one of the very first things I was taught by Dave Bryson. He was the head baker and confectioner at a famous bakery in Fife, and a great inspiration to me in my younger days.

Makes about 25 small bars

265ml (9½fl oz/generous 1 cup) ready-made coconut purée or unsweetened coconut milk
60g (2oz) invert sugar (see page 23)
450g (1lb) fine white chocolate, finely chopped
225g (8oz) desiccated (shredded, dried) coconut, lightly toasted
500g (1lb 2oz) tempered fine dark (bittersweet) chocolate (see pages 18–19), to coat

1 Put the coconut purée or coconut milk and invert sugar in a saucepan and bring to the boil. Gradually pour this over the white chocolate in a mixing bowl, stirring continuously to form an emulsion. Mix in the toasted coconut. Pour the coconut ganache into a 28 × 35cm (11 × 14 inch) deep-sided baking tray (sheet) lined with silicone (baking) paper. Leave to set overnight in a cool, dry area.

2 To finish, turn the ganache out of the baking tray (sheet) and cut into 25 small rectangles (about 7.5 × 2.5cm (3 × 1 inch) each), then use a dipping fork to coat in the tempered chocolate and decorate with the prongs of the fork. Leave to set fully in a cool, dry area. Store in an airtight container and consume within 1 week.

SEA SALT CARAMEL MOU

Salted caramel mou or soft caramel originates from Brittany, famous for its fleur de sel and butter.

Makes about 15–18 small bars

150ml (5fl oz/⅔ cup) whipping (pouring) cream
½ vanilla pod (bean), split lengthways
340g (11½oz/1½ cups) caster (superfine) sugar
35g (1¼oz) liquid glucose
140g (5oz/1⅓ sticks) sea salt butter, cut into cubes and at room temperature
500g (1lb 2oz) tempered fine dark (bittersweet) chocolate (see pages 18–19), to coat
5g (1 tsp) sea salt, to decorate

1 Put the cream in a pan. Scrape the seeds from the vanilla pod (bean) into the pan and drop in the empty pod. Bring to the boil. Cover with a lid, take off the heat and leave to infuse for 10–15 minutes. Discard the vanilla.

2 In a separate heated pan, gradually add the sugar and glucose and cook it slowly to form an amber caramel, about 15 minutes.

3 Slowly add the infused cream, mixing well. Cook the caramel to 110°C (230°F), add the butter, piece by piece, and continue to cook until the mixture reaches 125°C (257°F). Pour into a 25.5 × 30cm (10 × 12 inch) deep-sided silicone baking tin (pan) and leave to set overnight in a cool, dry area. Finish as for the Chocolate Coconut Bar *(see previous recipe)*, cutting into 15–18 small bars, and decorate with a sprinkling of sea salt.

CHOCOLATE CARAMEL MOU

A perfect caramel should be cooked until it's dark, red brown, with a light smoky haze coming from the pan.

Makes about 15–18 small bars

220ml (7½fl oz/scant 1 cup) whipping (pouring) cream
½ vanilla pod (bean), split lengthways
290g (10oz/1⅓ cups) caster (superfine) sugar
40g (1½oz) liquid glucose
20g (¾oz/1¾ tbsp) unsalted butter, cubed
100g (3½oz) fine dark (bittersweet) chocolate (63% cocoa solids), finely chopped
500g (1lb 2oz) tempered fine dark (bittersweet) chocolate (see pages 18–19)
25g (scant 1oz) cocoa nibs, finely chopped, to decorate

1 Put the cream in a pan. Scrape the seeds from the vanilla pod (bean) into the pan and drop in the empty pod. Bring to the boil. Cover with a lid, take off the heat and leave to infuse for 10–15 minutes. Discard the vanilla.

2 In a separate heated pan, gradually add the sugar and glucose and cook slowly to form an amber caramel, about 15 minutes. Slowly add the cream, mixing well. Cook the caramel to 110°C (230°F), add the butter and continue to cook until the mixture reaches 125°C (257°F). Add the chocolate and stir until melted. Pour into a 25.5 × 30cm (10 × 12 inch) deep-sided silicone baking tin (pan) and leave to set overnight. Finish as for the Chocolate Coconut Bar *(see far left)*, cutting into 15–18 small bars, and decorate with a sprinkling of chopped cocoa nibs.

CHOCOLATE MERINGUE

This is such a simple dish, made using the traditional French method.

Makes about 24 mini meringues

120g (4¼oz) egg whites (about 6 eggs)
180g (6oz/¾ cup) caster (superfine) sugar
60g (2oz/generous ⅓ cup) icing
   (powdered/pure) sugar, sifted
15g (½oz/1 tbsp) cocoa powder
20g (¾oz) cocoa nibs, roughly chopped
500g (1lb 2oz) tempered dark chocolate
   (see pages 18–19), for dipping

1 Preheat the oven to 110°C
(225°F/Gas ¼) and line a baking tray
(sheet) with silicone (baking) paper.
Put the egg whites in the bowl of
an electric mixer and whisk on a slow
speed, gradually adding the caster
(superfine) sugar and increasing the
speed. Continue to whisk until stiff
peaks form. Carefully fold in the icing
(powdered/pure) sugar and cocoa
powder – do not overwork the mixture.

2 Spoon into a piping (pastry) bag,
snip a hole in the end and pipe 3.5cm
(1½ inch) bulbs onto the tray. Sprinkle
with cocoa nibs and bake for 1½ hours,
lowering the oven to its lowest setting
(or leaving the door slightly ajar) halfway
through baking. Leave to cool and then
dip the bases in tempered chocolate.

RUM & RAISIN BOUCHÉE

*While with Marco Pierre White at The Restaurant we used to make a small
version of this for a tray of chocolates served with coffee – it was very classy.*

Makes 16 bouchées

125g (4½oz/¾ cup) raisins,
   washed and drained
75ml (2½fl oz/scant ⅓ cup) dark rum
220ml (7½fl oz/scant 1 cup) whipping
   (pouring) cream
30g (1oz) invert sugar
500g (1lb 2oz) fine dark (bittersweet)
   chocolate (65% cocoa solids),
   finely chopped
40g (1½oz/3 tbsp) unsalted butter, cut
   into cubes and at room temperature
500g (1lb 2oz) tempered fine dark
   (bittersweet) chocolate
   (see pages 18–19), to coat

1 Put the raisins in an airtight
container and add the rum. Seal and
and leave to marinate overnight.

2 Put the cream and invert sugar into
a saucepan, bring to the boil and then
leave to cool to 65–70°C (149–
158°F). Melt the chocolate over a
bain-marie (water bath) to about 45°C
(113°F), then gradually add the cream
to the chocolate, mixing continuously
to form an emulsion. Add the butter
and mix until smooth.

3 Mix in half of the soaked raisins
and any excess rum and then pour
the mixture into a shallow 18 × 18cm
(7 × 7 inch) silicone cake tin (pan) and
spoon the remaining raisins on top.
Leave to set in a cool, dry area, ideally
overnight, and then cut into 4 × 4cm
(1½ × 1½ inch) squares. Dip each
square in tempered chocolate, set aside
to fully set, then store in an airtight
container and eat within 1 week.

CHOCOLATE MACAROONS

Although considered a French delicacy, the known origins of macaroons are greatly debated. Pierre Desfontaines of the French patisserie, Ladurée, is usually credited with creating the Parisian macaroon – adapted from a recipe for a biscuit-based gateaux, which he changed to small almond cakes sandwiched together with a range of different-flavoured ganache.

Makes about 12–14 macaroons

½ quantity **Basic Ganache** *(see pages 22–23)*

For the macaroons
120g (4¼oz) egg whites (about 4 eggs)
125g (4½oz/1⅔ cups) ground almonds, sifted
125g (4½oz/¾ cup) icing (powdered/pure) sugar, sifted
25g (scant 1oz/¼ cup) cocoa powder
125g (4½oz/generous ½ cup) caster (superfine) sugar

1 To make the chocolate macaroons, put 60g (2oz) of the egg whites in a mixing bowl along with the ground almonds, icing (powdered/pure) sugar and cocoa powder and beat to a paste.

2 Put the remaining egg whites and the caster (superfine) sugar in a separate mixing bowl and beat with a whisk until smooth. Place the bowl over a bain-marie (water bath) and whisk until the meringue is quite hot at around 65°C (149°F). Transfer to the bowl of an electric mixer (or continue by hand) and continue to whisk until a stiff meringue forms and the mixture returns to room temperature. Using a spatula, fold the meringue into the paste until it is smooth.

3 Spoon the mixture into a piping (pastry) bag fitted with a 12mm (½ inch) plain nozzle (tip) and pipe an even number of 5cm (2 inch) diameter bulbs (you should get about 24–28) onto a baking tray (sheet) lined with a non-stick baking mat. Leave to dry out for 20–25 minutes. Meanwhile, preheat the oven to 150°C (300°F/Gas 2). Bake in the oven for 15 minutes. Reduce the temperature to 140°C (275°F/Gas 1) and cook for a further 6–8 minutes.

4 To assemble, use the dark chocolate ganache to sandwich 2 macaroon halves together, then leave to set for about 20 minutes. Store in a cool, dry area and eat within 2–3 days.

COFFEE MACAROONS

Macaroons have become incredibly popular in recent years. Pierre Hermé, the famous Parisian patissier is the King of Macaroons and has been at the forefront of their success since he opened his shops in the 1990s.

Makes about 12–14 macaroons

½ quantity **Basic Ganache** *(see pages 22–23)*, made by adding ½ tsp freshly ground coffee beans to the cream before boiling, leaving to infuse for 15 minutes, straining, adding the invert sugar and then boiling again and continue with the basic recipe

For the macaroons
120g (4½oz) egg whites (about 4 eggs)
8g (1 tsp) freeze-dried or instant coffee
125g (4½oz/1⅔ cups) ground almonds, sifted
125g (4½oz/¾ cup) icing (powdered/pure) sugar, sifted
125g (4½oz/generous ½ cup) caster (superfine) sugar

1 To make the coffee macaroons, place 60g (2oz) of the egg whites and the coffee in a mixing bowl for 15 minutes to allow the coffee to dissolve. Add the ground almonds and icing (powdered/pure) sugar and beat to a paste.

2 Put the remaining egg whites and the caster (superfine) sugar in a separate bowl and beat with a whisk until smooth. Place the bowl over a bain-marie (water bath) and whisk until the meringue is quite hot at around 65°C (149°F). Transfer to the bowl of an electric mixer (or continue by hand) and continue to whisk until a stiff meringue forms and the mixture returns to room temperature. Using a spatula, fold the meringue into the coffee paste until it is smooth.

3 Spoon the mixture into a piping (pastry) bag fitted with a 12mm (½ inch) plain nozzle (tip) and pipe an even number of 5cm (2 inch) diameter bulbs (you should get about 24–28) onto a baking tray (sheet) lined with a non-stick baking mat. Leave to dry out for 20–25 minutes. Meanwhile, preheat the oven to 150°C (300°F/Gas 2). Bake in the oven for 15 minutes. Reduce the temperature to 140°C (275°F/Gas 1) and cook for a further 6–8 minutes.

4 To assemble, use the coffee and chocolate ganache to sandwich 2 macaroon halves together, then leave to set for about 20 minutes. Store in a cool, dry area and eat within 2–3 days.

HAZELNUT & FEUILLANTINE CAKES

A little cake, with a nutty soft centre.

Makes 10–12 cakes

60g (2oz) fine dark (bittersweet) chocolate (63% cocoa solids), finely chopped
100g (3½oz/1 stick) unsalted butter, cut into cubes and softened
85g (3oz/generous ⅓ cup) caster (superfine) sugar
80g (2¾oz) whole eggs (about 1½ eggs)
50g (1¾oz/⅓ cup) plain (all-purpose) flour, sifted
85g (3oz/generous ½ cup) hazelnuts, chopped, plus extra to decorate
25g (scant 1oz) feuillantine wafers
500g (1lb 2oz) tempered fine milk chocolate (see pages 18–19), to coat

1 Preheat the oven to 180°C (350°F/Gas 4). Melt the chocolate over a bain-marie (water bath). Cream the butter in a bowl until light and fluffy, then add the melted chocolate and combine.

2 Whisk together the sugar and eggs over a bain-marie (water bath) to 50°C (122°C). Then whisk until it reaches the ribbon stage (see page 218). Mix into the chocolate. Fold in the flour, hazelnuts and feuillantine wafers and pipe or spoon into a 12-hole silicone mini-muffin mould. Bake in the oven for 12–15 minutes until risen and the cakes spring back when pressed. Leave to cool. Coat in the tempered chocolate, then decorate with the base of a piping nozzle (tip), sprinkle with the hazelnuts and leave to set. Store in an airtight container and eat within 1 week.

CHOCOLATE & PRALINE DACQUOISE
Hazelnut meringue sandwiched with a praline chocolate ganache.

Makes 12

½ quantity **Basic Ganache** (see pages 22–23), made using a mix of fine dark (bittersweet) and milk chocolate and by adding 175g (6oz) **Praline Paste** (see pages 158–159) in with the butter in the final steps

For the hazelnut meringue
150g (5½oz/scant 1 cup) icing (powdered/pure) sugar, sifted
75g (2½oz/1 cup) ground almonds
75g (2½oz/1 cup) ground hazelnuts
45g (1½oz/⅓ cup) plain (all-purpose) flour, sifted
225g (8oz) egg whites (about 7½ eggs)
90g (3oz/generous ⅓ cup) caster (superfine) sugar
75g (2½oz/¾ cup) flaked almonds

1 Preheat the oven to 160°C (325°F/Gas 3), line a baking tray (sheet) with a non-stick baking mat and lightly grease six 6cm (2½ inch) metal rings or cutters. To make the hazelnut meringue, mix together the icing (powdered/pure) sugar, ground almonds and hazelnuts and flour in a bowl.

2 In an electric mixer, slowly whisk the egg whites, gradually adding the sugar and increasing the speed. Mix until the meringue forms a firm peak. Gradually fold in the dry ingredients. Spoon the mixture into a piping (pastry) bag, snip a hole in the end and pipe the meringue mix into the rings. Level off with a palette knife before removing the rings and repeating until you have about

24 meringue discs. Sprinkle the flaked almonds on top and lightly dust with icing sugar. Bake in the oven for 20–25 minutes and then leave to cool.

3 To assemble the dacquoise, spoon the ganache into a piping (pastry) bag, snip off the end and pipe swirls onto half of the meringue discs. Top each swirl with another meringue disc. Best eaten the same day.

CHOCOLATE CROQUANTS

This is a simple recipe with the three elements creating fantastic textural contrasts.

Makes about 20–25 croquants

For the sablé pastry
195g (6¾oz/2 sticks) unsalted butter,
  cut into cubes and softened
100g (3½oz/⅔ cup) icing (powdered/
  pure) sugar, sifted
100g (3½oz/1¼ cups) ground almonds
165g (5½oz/ generous 1 cup) plain
  (all-purpose) flour, sifted
1g (a pinch) salt

For the croquant wafers
60g (2oz/5 tbsp) unsalted butter
7g (1 tsp) liquid glucose
75g (2½oz/⅓ cup) caster (superfine) sugar
75g (2½oz) cocoa nibs
10g (¼oz) pistachio nuts, chopped

For the pistachio ganache
300ml (½ pint/1¼ cups) whipping
  (pouring) cream
30g (1oz) **Pistachio Paste** (*see page 52*)
250g (9oz) fine dark (bittersweet)
  chocolate (63% cocoa solids),
  finely chopped
20g (¾oz/1¾ tbsp) unsalted butter

1 To make the pastry, mix together the butter and icing (powdered/pure) sugar until light and creamy. Add the almonds, flour and salt and mix until smooth. Put the pastry on a floured tray (sheet), wrap with cling film (plastic wrap) and chill for 1 hour.

2 The dough will be very soft, so roll it out between two sheets of silicone (baking) paper and chill for 20 minutes. Meanwhile, preheat the oven to 160°C (325°F/Gas 3), line a baking tray (sheet) with silicone (baking) paper and grease five 5cm (2 inch) metal rings. Use a 5cm (2 inch) cutter to cut out 5 circles from the pastry and place them in the

rings on the tray. Bake for about 15 minutes (removing the rings halfway through cooking) until golden brown. Repeat until you have about 20–25 circles. Leave to cool. Raise the oven temperature to 180°C (350°F/Gas 4).

3 To make the wafers, melt the butter in a pan over a low heat and add the glucose and sugar. Stir until the mixture combines and then take off the heat – be careful not to overmix. Add the cocoa nibs and pistachios. Spoon 2cm (¾ inch) bulbs onto a baking tray (sheet) lined with silicone (baking) paper, leaving 5cm (2 inch) gaps to allow the wafer to spread. Cook in the oven for about 10 minutes until golden. Leave

to cool slightly, then use a 5cm (2 inch) round cutter to cut out 20–25 circles from the wafers. Use straight away or store in an airtight container.

4 To make the ganache, put the cream and pistachio paste in a pan, bring to the boil and then gradually pour over the chopped chocolate in a bowl, mixing to form an emulsion. Add the butter and mix until smooth. Leave to firm for about 1 hour.

5 To assemble, spoon the ganache into a pastry (piping) bag with an 8mm (⅓ inch) plain nozzle (tip) and pipe 7 ganache bulbs on each base and top with a wafer. Best eaten the same day.

BLACKCURRANT TEACAKES

Teacakes can be quite sweet – we have used blackcurrant to balance the flavours.

Makes about 20–25 teacakes

500g (1lb 2oz) tempered fine dark
   (bittersweet) chocolate
   (see pages 18–19), to coat
1 tbsp blackcurrant powder
   (see page 224), to decorate

For the blackcurrant purée
50ml (1¾fl oz/3 tbsp) water
50g (1¾oz) caster (superfine) sugar
500g (1lb 2oz) blackcurrants, washed
   and stalks removed
10ml (¾ tbsp) lemon juice

For the blackcurrant jam
250g (9oz) blackcurrants,
   washed and stalks removed
250g (9oz) blackcurrant purée
   (see above)
200g (7oz/scant 1 cup) jam sugar
15ml (1 tbsp) lemon juice
OR
10g (¼oz) ready-made blackcurrant jam
   per teacake

For the rich sweet pastry
175g (6oz/1¾ sticks) unsalted butter,
   cut into cubes
250g (9oz/1⅔ cups) plain (all-purpose)
   flour, sifted
90g (3oz/generous ½ cup) icing
   (powdered/pure) sugar
A pinch of salt
40g (1½oz) egg yolks (about 2 eggs)

For the marshmallow
9g (¼oz) leaf gelatine
100g (3½oz) blackcurrant purée
   (see above)
40g (1½oz) egg whites (about 2 eggs)
225g (8oz/1 cup) caster
   (superfine) sugar
55ml (2fl oz/¼) water
40g (1½oz) liquid glucose

Note: Make the purée, jam and
pastry dough in advance and store
in airtight containers until needed.

First, make the blackcurrant purée:

1 Put the water and sugar in a pan,
bring to the boil and then leave to
cool. Put the blackcurrants in a food
processor and add the sugar syrup and
lemon juice. Blitz to a smooth purée
and then pass through a fine sieve
(strainer). Store in an airtight container
in the fridge until needed.

Second, make the blackcurrant jam:

2 Put the blackcurrants, purée and
sugar in a large pan and bring to the
boil. Continue to simmer, stirring, over
a low heat. After about 5 minutes, test
if the jam has reached setting point;
take your jam off the heat, spoon a
small amount onto a cold plate and
leave to cool. If it has a crinkled skin
when you push it then it is ready, if not
then contiue to cook while continuously
stirring. Once the jam reaches setting
point, stir in the lemon juice whilst still
over the heat and leave to cool.

Next, make the rich sweet pastry:

3 Crumb together the butter and
flour in a large bowl with your hands
until there are no lumps. Add the icing
(powdered/pure) sugar and salt, then
gradually mix in the eggs until the
mixture comes together in a dough.
Roll the pastry into a ball, wrap with
cling film (plastic wrap) and rest for at
least 1 hour in the fridge.

4 Line a baking tray (sheet) with
a non-stick baking mat. Roll out the
pastry to 4mm (⅛ inch) thick and use
a 5cm (2 inch) round cutter to cut out
20–25 circles. Place on the tray (sheet)
and leave to rest for 30 minutes in
the fridge. Preheat the oven to 180°C
(350°F/Gas 4) and bake for 15–18
minutes until golden. Leave to cool.

Now, the marshmallow:

5 Soak the gelatine in enough water
to just cover it for a few minutes
until it is soft and then drain. Put the
blackcurrant purée in a pan and bring to
the boil. Add the drained gelatine, stir
and pass through a fine sieve (strainer).

6 Put the egg whites in the bowl of an
electric mixer set on a low speed and
start whisking. In separate saucepan
boil the sugar and water, add the liquid
glucose and cook to 121°C (250°F).
Gradually pour this onto the egg
whites, while continuing to mix. Once
all the sugar is incorporated, continue
to mix for another 3–4 minutes.
Reheat the blackcurrant purée and
gelatine mixture and gradually pour
this into the meringue. Continue to
whisk until the meringue reaches a full
peak and cools down.

To assemble & finish the teacake:

7 Put the sweet pastry discs onto a
non-stick baking tray (sheet). Spoon the
blackcurrant jam into a piping (pastry)
bag fitted with a 12mm (½ inch) plain
nozzle (tip). Pipe a generous bulb of
jam in the centre of each disc. Spoon
the marshmallow into another piping
(pastry) bag fitted with a 15mm (¾
inch) plain nozzle (tip) and pipe a large
bulb on top of the jam. Leave the
partially made teacakes to set for about
2 hours in a cool, dry area.

8 Using a dipping fork, dip the
teacakes into the tempered chocolate
sponge-side down ensuring they are
fully covered. Sprinkle over some
blackcurrant powder and leave to set
in a cool, dry area. Store in an airtight
container and eat within 1 week.

ORANGE TEACAKES

These cakes are all about nostalgia – they are a tribute to my childhood memories. We have added an orange ganache to give more depth to this classic cake, and we also make our own marmalade as I love having chunky orange pieces.

Makes about 25 teacakes

25 chocolate discs measuring 4.5cm
(1¾ inch), made using the Flat Sheet
Technique (see page 157)
500g (1lb 2oz) tempered fine dark
(bittersweet) chocolate
(see pages 18–19), to coat

For the orange marmalade

4 Seville oranges
(weighing about 450g/1lb in total)
1 lemon
1 litre (1¾ pints/4 cups) water
800g (1¾lb/4⅓ cups) caster
(superfine) sugar
50g (1¾oz/¼ cup) dark soft brown sugar
OR
10g (¼oz) shop-bought marmalade
per teacake

For the orange dust

Finely grated zest of 1 orange

For the Genoise sponge

90g (3oz) egg whites (about 3 eggs)
90g (3oz/generous ⅓ cup) caster
(superfine) sugar
100g (3½oz) egg yolks (about 5 eggs)
90g (3oz/scant ⅔ cup) plain
(all-purpose) flour

For the orange ganache

500ml (16fl oz/2 cups) orange juice
½ vanilla pod (bean), split lengthways
225g (8oz) fine dark (bittersweet)
chocolate (66% cocoa solids),
finely chopped

Notes:

• Make the marmalade, orange dust
and sponge in advance and store
in airtight containers until needed.
The sponge could also be frozen.
• The ganache should be made
just before you assemble the
teacakes.

First, make the orange marmalade:

1 Remove the orange peel in long
strips using a peeler. Trim any white
pith from the peel, finely slice and
place in a muslin bag. Slice the oranges
and lemon and place into a large pan.
Add the water, both sugars and the
orange peel muslin bag. Simmer over a
low heat, uncovered, for about 2 hours
until the pith is tender. Remove the
muslin bag and set aside to drain.

2 Line a colander with layers of muslin
and place it over a bowl. Tip in the
contents of the pan and leave to strain
for about 30 minutes. Squeeze out all
the liquid, return it to the pan along
with the peel from the muslin. Bring
to the boil and cook for 5 minutes
until it reaches 104°C (219°F), stirring
frequently. To test the marmalade is
at setting point, spoon a small amount
onto a cold plate and leave to cool. If
it sets, take the marmalade off the heat
and leave to cool. If it doesn't set, try
again after a few more minutes.

Second, make the orange dust:

3 Preheat the oven to 110°C (225°F/
Gas ¼). Sprinkle the finely grated zest
on a baking tray (sheet) lined with a
non-stick baking mat and put in the
oven for 1–2 hours to dry. Leave to
cool and store in an airtight container.

Third, make the Genoise sponge:

4 Put the egg whites in the bowl
of an electric mixer and whisk until
stiff. Gradually add the sugar while
continuing to whisk. Slowly increase
the speed until a soft peak meringue
forms. Continue whisking and
gradually add the egg yolks.

5 Carefully fold in the flour and
spread the mixture into a 25.5 × 30cm
(10 × 12 inch) deep-sided baking tray
(sheet) lined with a non-stick baking
mat. Bake for 18–20 minutes, or until
the sponge springs back when pressed.
Leave to cool and store in an airtight
container until needed.

The next day, make the orange ganache:

6 Put the orange juice in a saucepan.
Scrape the seeds from the vanilla pod
(bean) into the pan and drop in the
empty pod. Bring to the boil. Boil,
uncovered, until it has reduced to
200ml (7fl oz/generous ¾ cup). Pass
through a sieve (strainer) into a bowl
containing the chocolate (remove and
discard the vanilla). Mix to form a
smooth emulsion. Leave to firm.

To assemble (see above right):

7 Cut out 5cm (2 inch) diameter discs
from the Genoise sponge and place on
a tray. You will need about 25.

8 Spoon the ganache into a piping
(pastry) bag fitted with an 8mm (⅓ inch)
plain nozzle (tip). Pipe a ring of ganache
around the edge of each sponge and
then spoon the marmalade into the
centre. Place a chocolate disc on top
of each one.

9 Using a dipping fork, dip the
teacakes into the tempered chocolate
sponge-side down ensuring they are
fully covered. Decorate with the fork
and sprinkle over some orange dust.
Leave to set in a cool, dry area. Store
in an airtight container and eat within
1 week.

CAKES &
BISCUITS

CHOCOLATE MADELEINES

When I worked for Marco we would bake these little French treats to order for petit fours as they are best eaten as fresh as possible.

Makes about 20 cakes

15g (½oz) fine dark (bittersweet) chocolate (70% cocoa solids), roughly chopped

115g (4oz/1 stick plus 1 tbsp) unsalted butter, plus a little extra, softened, for greasing the mould

115g (4oz/¾ cup) plain (all-purpose) flour, plus a little extra for dusting the mould

20g (¾oz/1 tbsp) cocoa powder

3g (½ tsp) baking powder

135g (5oz/scant ⅔ cup) caster (superfine) sugar

175g (6oz) egg yolks (about 9 eggs), beaten

1 Grease with butter and lightly flour a 12-hole madeleine mould (see page 224). Melt the chocolate over a bain-marie (water bath) until it reaches 45°C (113°F) and leave to cool. Melt the butter in a saucepan and also leave to cool. Sift the flour, cocoa powder and baking powder into a bowl and then mix in the sugar. Add the dry ingredients to the beaten egg yolks in a large bowl and mix with a wooden spoon until smooth. Gradually add the melted butter, being careful not to beat in air. Then mix in the melted chocolate. Cover the bowl with cling film (plastic wrap) and leave to rest for at least 30 minutes in a cool place.

2 When you are ready to cook the madeleines, preheat the oven to 200°C (400°F/Gas 6). Pipe or spoon the mixture into the prepared mould and bake in the preheated oven for about 12–15 minutes until risen and the cakes spring back when pressed. Repeat the baking process with the remaining mixture. Remove from the mould and cool on a wire rack. Best served immediately.

> **Note:** You will need a 12-hole madeleine mould *(see page 224).*

MOLLEAUX AU CHOCOLAT

This is a moist and tender chocolate cake, which is a dessert in its own right. It is also great served with fresh raspberries or cherries.

Makes 8–10 cakes

85g (3oz/generous ½ cup) plain (all-purpose) flour, sifted

3g (½ tsp) baking powder

100g (3½oz) fine dark (bittersweet) chocolate (63% cocoa solids), roughly chopped

100g (3½oz/1 stick) unsalted butter

75g (2½oz/⅓ cup) caster (superfine) sugar

100g (3½oz) whole eggs (about 2 eggs)

15g (½oz) cocoa nibs

> **Note:** You will need two silicone 6-hole muffin moulds *(see page 224).*

1 Preheat the oven to 180°C (350°F/Gas 4). Line 8–10 of the holes in two silicone 6-hole muffin moulds with 12cm (5 inch) square of parchment paper.

2 Sift the flour and baking powder into a bowl. Melt the chocolate over a bain-marie (water bath) to 45°C (113°F). Put the butter and sugar in a bowl and cream together in an electric mixer or by hand until light and fluffy. Add the melted chocolate and mix until smooth. Gradually add the eggs until fully incorporated. Fold in the flour and baking powder.

3 Spoon the mixture into the muffin moulds, liberally sprinkle with cocoa nibs and bake in the preheated oven for 16–18 minutes until risen and the cakes spring back when pressed. Leave to cool before removing from the moulds, but keep the parchment paper around each cake.

CHOCOLATE FIG CAKES

The combination of figs and chocolate is surprisingly under-used as they work together so well. These cakes are rich and deep in flavour and the figs add a beautiful element of texture.

Makes about 20 cakes

For the figs

200ml (7fl oz/generous ¾ cup) red wine

40g (1½oz) caster (superfine) sugar

A pinch of grated nutmeg

1 cinnamon stick

½ vanilla pod (bean), split lengthways

200g (7oz) semi-dried figs, stalks removed and cut into 1cm (½ inch) dice

For the cake

155g (5½oz) fine dark (bittersweet) chocolate (70% cocoa solids), finely chopped

65g (2oz/scant ½ cup) plain (all-purpose) flour

80g (3oz/¾ cup) cocoa powder

3g (½ tsp) baking powder

150g (5½oz/1½ sticks) unsalted butter, softened, plus a little melted for greasing the moulds

215g (7½oz/scant 1 cup) caster (superfine) sugar

310g (10½oz) eggs (about 6 eggs)

30g (1oz) honey

120ml (4fl oz/½ cup) whipping (pouring) cream

To decorate

100g (3½oz) semi-dried figs, stalks removed, cut into 1cm (½ inch) dice

25g (scant 1oz) hazelnuts, chopped

1 To make the figs, put the red wine, sugar, nutmeg and cinnamon in a saucepan. Scrape the seeds from the split vanilla pod (bean) in to the pan and drop in the empty pod too. Bring to the boil. Add the figs and cook over a low heat for 4–5 minutes and then leave to cool. Cover and leave to marinate in the fridge overnight.

2 Grease a 25-cell silicone mould with melted butter. Preheat the oven to 180°C (350°F/Gas 4). Drain the excess liquid (and cinnamon stick and vanilla pod) from the figs and set aside. The left-over liquid can be used to poach any other fruits, just remove the cinnamon stick and vanilla pod. Melt the chocolate over a bain-marie (water bath) until it reaches 45°C (113°F). Sift the flour, cocoa powder and baking powder into a bowl. Put the butter and sugar in the bowl of an electric mixer and cream together until light and fluffy. Gradually add the eggs and honey and then add in the melted chocolate and mix until smooth. Alternatively, mix by hand in a large mixing bowl.

3 Warm the cream to around 45°C (113°F) and add to the cake mix, then fold in the soaked figs and the dry ingredients. Spoon into the prepared mould until three-quarters full and decorate with the chopped figs and hazelnuts.

4 Bake in the preheated oven for 18–20 minutes until risen and the cakes spring back when pressed. Leave to cool before removing from the mould.

Note: You will need a silicone mould with 25 cells each measuring 8 × 3 × 3cm (3½ × 1 × 1 inch) *(see page 224).*

CHOCOLATE & PISTACHIO CAKE

Chocolate and pistachios go together so well and the cocoa nibs give a fantastically crunchy crust leaving the inside moist and succulent.

Makes 2 x 500g (1lb 2oz) cakes

30g (1oz) cocoa nibs, roughly chopped

For the apricot confit
100g (3½oz) soft dried apricots,
   chopped into 5mm (¼ inch) pieces
100ml (3½fl oz/generous ⅓ cup)
   orange juice
2 tbsp Kirsch

For the chocolate cake
250g (9oz) fine dark (bittersweet)
   chocolate (66% cocoa solids),
   finely chopped
250g (9oz/2½ sticks) unsalted butter,
   softened, plus a little extra, for greasing
   the tins (pans)
175g (6oz/¾ cup) caster
   (superfine) sugar
200g (7oz) whole eggs
   (about 4 eggs), beaten
75g (2½oz/½ cup) plain (all-purpose)
   flour, sifted

For the pistachio cake
60g (2oz/5 tbsp) unsalted butter
25g (scant 1oz) plain (all-purpose) flour
25g (scant 1oz) cornflour (cornstarch)
100g (3½oz) Pistachio Paste
   (see page 52)
100g (3½oz/⅔ cup) icing (powdered/
   pure) sugar
140g (5oz) whole eggs (about 3 eggs)
10ml (2 tsp) Kirsch

> **Note:** You will need two
> 18 × 8cm (7 × 3½ inch) loaf
> tins (pans) *(see page 224).*

1 For the apricot confit, put the apricots and orange juice into a saucepan and bring to the boil. Remove from the heat and leave to cool completely. Add the Kirsch, cover and leave to soak overnight in the fridge.

2 Preheat the oven to 180°C (350°F/Gas 4). Grease two 18 × 8cm (7 × 3½ inch) loaf tins (pans) with soft unsalted butter and coat the sides with the cocoa nibs.

3 To make the chocolate cake, melt the chocolate over a bain-marie (water bath) until it reaches 45°C (113°F). Put the butter and sugar in a bowl and cream together until light and creamy. Add the melted chocolate and mix until smooth. Gradually add the eggs until fully incorporated. Fold in the flour.

4 To make the pistachio cake, melt the butter in a saucepan and then let it cool to 39°C (102°F). Sift the flour and cornflour (cornstarch) into a bowl. Put the pistachio paste, icing (powdered/pure) sugar and eggs in the bowl of an electric mixer and beat together for 5 minutes until light and aerated (or mix by hand in a large bowl). Fold in the flour and cornflour (cornstarch), and before it is fully combined, mix the melted butter with a small amount of the mixture in a separate bowl. Fold it back into the mix together with the kirsch.

5 Spoon 300g (10oz) of the chocolate cake mix into each loaf tin (pan) and use a palette knife to make sure the sides of the mould are lined with the chocolate cake mix. Place 100g (3½oz) of apricot confit down the centre of the loaf tin (pan) and then spoon 175g (6oz) of the pistachio cake mixture on top of this. Level off and divide the remaining chocolate cake mix between the two tins.

6 Bake in the preheated oven for 30–35minutes until the cake is lightly springy when pressed in the centre. Leave to cool, remove from the tins and allow to cool completely. Cut into slices to serve.

RUM & RAISIN CAKES

This is an easy cake to make and is fantastic as an afternoon pick-me-up. The trick is to make sure you marinate your raisins for 24 hours before baking.

Makes about 20 cakes

100g (3½oz/scant ⅔ cup) raisins
45ml (1¾fl oz/3 tbsp) dark rum
100g (3½oz) fine dark (bittersweet)
   chocolate (65% cocoa solids),
   finely chopped
120g (4½oz/1¼ sticks) unsalted butter,
   cut into cubes and softened
60g (2oz) egg yolks (about 3 eggs)
65g (2oz/scant ½ cup) plain
   (all-purpose) flour, sifted
90g (3oz) egg whites (about 3 eggs)
100g (3½oz/scant ½ cup) caster
   (superfine) sugar

Note: You will need a 24-hole silicone mini muffin mould *(see page 224).*

1 Wash the raisins in warm water (this will open them up a bit and allow the rum to penetrate). Put the raisins and rum in a bowl, cover and leave to soak overnight.

2 Preheat the oven to 180°C (350°F/Gas 4). Melt the chocolate over a bain-marie (water bath) until it reaches 45˚C (113°F). Put the butter in a bowl and cream until light and fluffy. Add the melted chocolate and mix until smooth, then gradually mix in the egg yolks followed by the flour, raisins and rum

3 In another bowl, slowly beat the egg whites until stiff. Gradually add the sugar while continuing to beat. Slowly increase the speed until soft peaks form. Fold one-third of the meringue into the chocolate mixture, mix until smooth and fold in the remainder.

4 Spoon the mixture into a 24-hole silicone mini muffin mould until about 20 of the holes are three-quarters full. Bake in the preheated oven for about 12–15 minutes until risen and the centre of the cakes spring back. Leave to cool before removing from the mould.

CHESTNUT & SESAME BROWNIES

A Japanese take on a classic. The chestnut is a delicate flavour complementing the chocolate, while the sesame adds an interestingly nutty texture.

Makes about 12 brownies

70g (2½oz) white sesame seeds
170g (6oz) fine dark (bittersweet)
   chocolate (70% cocoa solids),
   finely chopped
220g (8oz/2¼ sticks) unsalted butter, cut
   into cubes and softened
300g (10oz/1⅓ cups) caster
   (superfine) sugar
200g (7oz) whole eggs (about 4 eggs)
1g (¼ tsp) salt
80g (2¾oz/½ cup) plain (all-purpose)
   flour, sifted
120g (4¼oz) tinned candied chestnuts,
   roughly chopped

1 Preheat the oven to 180°C (350°F/Gas 4). Line a deep 28 × 22 × 4cm (11 × 8½ × 1½ inch) cake tin (pan) with silicone (baking) paper. Put the sesame seeds into a frying pan (skillet) over a moderate heat and lightly toast them, stirring continuously.

2 Melt the chocolate over a bain-marie (water bath) until it reaches 45°C (113°F). Put the butter and sugar in a bowl and cream together until light and fluffy. Gradually add the eggs and salt and beat until fully incorporated.

3 Add the melted chocolate and mix until smooth. Fold in the flour, chestnuts and half of the toasted sesame seeds and pour the mixture into the prepared tin (pan). Sprinkle over the remaining sesame seeds.

4 Bake in the oven for about 30 minutes until a crust forms and it is slightly springy in the centre. Leave to cool and cut into squares.

Note: You will need a deep 28 × 22 × 4cm (11 × 8½ × 1½ inch) cake tin (pan) *(see page 224).*

FLORENTINE SABLÉS

This has been a firm favourite at our Richmond store for a long time. The sablé base adds another dimension to the florentine and the cocoa nibs work to overcome the sweetness of the caramel.

Makes about 16 florentines

For the chocolate sablé base
250g (9oz/1⅔ cups) plain
  (all-purpose) flour
50g (1¾oz/½ cup) cocoa powder
185g (6½oz/1¾ sticks) unsalted butter,
  cut into cubes and softened
140g (5oz/generous ¾ cup) icing
  (powdered/pure) sugar
25g (scant 1oz) whole egg (about
  ½ an egg)
20g (¾oz/generous ¼ cup)
  ground almonds

For the topping
20ml (1½ tbsp) whipping
  (pouring) cream
65g (2¼oz/5 tbsp)
  unsalted butter, softened
65g (2¼oz/scant ⅓ cup)
  caster (superfine) sugar
65g (2¼oz) liquid glucose
80g (2¾oz) flaked almonds
50g (1¾oz) cocoa nibs

> **Note:** You will need an
> 11 × 35cm (4½ × 14 inch)
> rectangular tart frame
> *(see page 224).*

1 To make the chocolate sablé base, line a baking tray (sheet) with a non-stick baking mat. Sift the flour and cocoa powder into a bowl. Put the butter and sugar in a separate bowl and cream together until light and fluffy.

2 Gradually mix in the egg and then fold in the dry ingredients. Do not overwork. Roll the pastry into a ball, place onto a lightly floured baking tray (sheet), wrap loosely in cling film (plastic wrap) and chill for 30 minutes.

3 Roll the dough out to an 11 × 35cm (4½ × 14 inch) rectangle that is 1cm (½ inch) thick on a lightly floured surface. Pierce lightly with a fork to make small holes in the dough to let steam escape during baking – this helps the dough to remain flat and even. Carefully place the rectangle on a baking tray (sheet) lined with silicone (baking) paper and place a 11 × 35cm (4½ × 14 inch) rectangular tart frame *(see page 224)* on top. Chill for at least 30 minutes in the fridge.

4 Preheat the oven to 180°C (350°F/Gas 4). To make the topping, put the cream, butter, sugar and glucose into a saucepan and bring to the boil. Remove from the heat and add the sliced almonds and cocoa nibs.

5 Bake the chocolate sablé base in the oven for about 20 minutes. Remove from the oven and pour the topping mixture over the sablé and spread evenly. Increase the oven temperature to 200°C (400°F/Gas 6) and bake for a further 10 minutes until golden. Leave to partially cool, remove the frame and cut into 5.5cm (2¼ inch) squares.

CHOCOLATE FINANCIERS WITH YUZU GANACHE

I add the soft yuzu (Japanese citrus fruit) ganache to the centre of our chocolate financiers to make the cakes that bit more indulgent. If you can't get hold of fresh yuzu zest, you can substitute with any other citrus fruit.

Makes about 12 cakes

For the chocolate financiers
220g (8oz/2¼ sticks) unsalted butter
20g (¾oz) fine dark (bittersweet)
   chocolate (66% cocoa solids),
   finely chopped
250g (9oz/1½ cups) icing
   (powdered/pure) sugar
20g (¾oz/1 tbsp) cocoa powder
80g (2¾oz/½ cup) plain
   (all-purpose) flour
120g (4¼oz/1½ cups) ground almonds
240g (9oz) egg whites (about 8 eggs)
25g (scant 1oz) **Orange Marmalade**
   (see page 126)

For the yuzu ganache
110ml (3½fl oz/½ cup) whipping
   (pouring) cream
2g (½ tsp) yuzu
   (Japanese citrus fruit) zest
125g (4½oz) fine dark (bittersweet)
   chocolate (66% cocoa solids),
   finely chopped
15g (½oz) unsalted butter

Edible gold leaf, to decorate (optional)

Note: You will need a 12-hole silicone financier mould *(see page 224).*

---

1 Preheat the oven to 180°C (350°F/Gas 4). To make the chocolate financiers, in a saucepan, bring the butter to the boil over a low heat, stirring occasionally. Cook it until the butter turns nut brown (about 15 minutes), remove from the heat and leave to cool for about 45 minutes. Meanwhile, melt the chocolate over a bain-marie (water bath) until it reaches 45°C (113°F).

2 Sift the icing (powdered/pure) sugar, cocoa powder and flour into a bowl and mix in the ground almonds and egg whites. Add the melted butter, melted chocolate and marmalade and beat until smooth.

3 Pipe or spoon the mixture into a silicone baking mould with oval divisions, each with a recess in the centre, and bake in the preheated oven for about 15–18 minutes until risen and firm to the touch. Leave to cool before removing from the mould.

4 To make the yuzu ganache, put the cream and yuzu zest into a saucepan and bring to the boil. Take off the heat and leave to cool until it reaches 70°C (158°F). Melt the chocolate over a bain-marie (water bath) until it reaches 45°C (113°F), then gradually add the cooled cream to the chocolate. Continue to mix to form an emulsion. Add the butter and continue to mix until fully incorporated.

5 Pipe the ganache into the centre of the financiers. Decorate with gold leaf (if using) and leave to set.

CHOCOLATE CAKE

This is made with dark chocolate, not cocoa powder, to give it added moisture.

Makes 2 x 500g (1lb 2oz) cakes

200g (7oz) fine dark (bittersweet) chocolate (70% cocoa solids), chopped
180g (6½oz/1¾ sticks) unsalted butter, cut into cubes, plus a little extra, softened, for greasing the tins (pans)
125g (4½oz) egg yolks (about 6 eggs)
200g (7oz) egg whites (about 7 eggs)
225g (8oz/1 cup) caster (superfine) sugar
A pinch of salt
100g (3½oz/⅔ cup) plain (all-purpose) flour, sifted
75g (2½oz/1 cup) ground almonds

1 Preheat the oven to 180°C (350°F/Gas 4). Lightly grease the tins (pans) with butter and line the bases with silicone (baking) paper. Melt the chocolate over a bain-marie (water bath) until it reaches 45°C (113°F). Add the butter to the melted chocolate and allow it to melt. Mix until the butter is fully incorporated.

2 In a separate bowl, beat the egg yolks and half the sugar by hand until light and smooth. In a mixing bowl, whisk together the egg whites with the remaining sugar to form a soft peak meringue. Mix the egg yolk and sugar mixture into the melted chocolate and fold in the flour and ground almonds. Then fold in the meringue in two stages.

3 Pour the mixture into the tins (pans) and bake in the preheated oven. After 10 minutes, when the cakes start to form a skin, score down the centre of the cakes with a sharp knife. Continue to cook for another 35 minutes until the cakes are slightly springy in the centres. Leave to cool before removing from the tins (pans).

Note: You will need two 18 x 8cm (7 x 3½ inch) loaf tins (pans) (see page 224).

MATCHA & CHOCOLATE SHORTBREAD

Being Scottish I love a bit of shortbread and Suzue being Japanese loves matcha (green tea powder), so it felt natural to combine the two.

Makes about 25 shortbread

185g (6½oz/1¼ cups) plain (all-purpose) flour, sifted
125g (4½oz/1¼ sticks) unsalted butter, cut into cubes, at room temperature
60g (2oz/¼ cup) caster (superfine) sugar
7g (1 tsp) matcha (green tea powder), plus extra for dusting
500g (1lb 2oz) tempered fine dark (bittersweet) chocolate (see pages 18–19), to coat

1 Preheat the oven to 160°C (325°F/Gas 3). Put all the ingredients, except the tempered chocolate, into a bowl and mix until the ingredients come together in a dough.

2 Remove from the bowl. Roll the dough to 5mm (¼ inch) thick on a lightly floured surface. Cut into 4cm (1½ inch) squares and transfer to a baking tray (sheet) lined with a non-stick baking mat. Leave to rest for at least 1 hour in the fridge.

3 Bake in the preheated oven for 20–25 minutes until lightly golden. Remove from the baking tray (sheet) and leave to cool. Dip in the tempered dark (bittersweet) chocolate and dust with matcha powder.

Makes about 15 rosettes

170g (6oz/generous 1 cup) plain
  (all-purpose) flour
10g (¼oz) cocoa powder
160g (5½oz/1⅓ sticks) unsalted butter,
  cut into cubes and softened
65g (2¼oz/generous ⅓ cup) icing
  (powdered/pure) sugar
30ml (1 fl oz) milk

For the cinnamon ganache
150ml (5fl oz/⅔ cup) whipping
  (pouring) cream
⅓ cinnamon stick
125g (4½oz) fine dark (bittersweet)
  chocolate (66% cocoa solids),
  finely chopped
12g (⅓oz) unsalted butter, cut into
  cubes and at room temperature

CHOCOLATE ROSETTES WITH CINNAMON GANACHE

We use cinnamon bark to infuse the cream rather than powder as it's cleaner on the palette and you'll get a smoother ganache.

1 For the rosettes, preheat the oven to 180°C (350°F/Gas 4). Sift the flour and cocoa powder into a bowl. Put the butter into a separate bowl and beat until soft. Sift in the icing (powdered/pure) sugar and beat together until light and fluffy. Gradually beat in the milk and then fold in the flour and cocoa powder.

2 Spoon the mixture into a piping (pastry) bag fitted with a 10mm (½ inch) star nozzle (tip). Pipe the dough into about thirty 3.5cm (1½ inch) diameter circles onto a baking tray (sheet) lined with a non-stick baking mat. Bake in the preheated oven for 20 minutes. Leave to cool.

3 For the ganache, put the cream and cinnamon stick in a saucepan and bring to the boil. Take off the heat, cover with cling film (plastic wrap) and leave to infuse for 30 minutes. Put the chocolate into a bowl. Bring the cream back to the boil and strain onto the chocolate, mixing with a spatula until the mixture is smooth. Add the butter and mix to form a smooth emulsion. Leave the ganache to firm for 1 hour, then spoon into a piping (pastry) bag fitted with a 10mm (½ inch) star nozzle (tip) and pipe a swirl onto the flat side of half of the rosettes. Top with the remaining rosettes, flat side down.

CHOCOLATE BRETONS

Originating in Brittany these biscuits are similar to shortbread, but the addition of egg yolks makes them richer and more crumbly.

Makes about 12 bretons

15g (½oz) fine dark (bittersweet)
  chocolate (70% cocoa solids), chopped
250g (9oz/2½ sticks) unsalted butter
150g (5½oz/scant 1 cup) icing
  (powdered/pure) sugar, sifted
60g (2oz) egg yolks (about 3 eggs)
160g (5½oz/generous 1 cup) plain (all-
  purpose) flour
30g (1oz/1¼ cup) cocoa powder
50g (1¾oz/⅔ cup) ground almonds
2g (¼ tsp) sea salt
Egg wash (made from 20g (¾oz) egg,
  6ml (½ tbsp) milk and a pinch of salt)

> **Note:** You will need twelve 6cm (2½ inch) tartlet rings.

1 Melt the chocolate over a bain-marie (water bath). Put the butter and sugar into a bowl and beat until it is very light and soft. Gradually add the egg yolks and then the melted chocolate. Sift the flour and cocoa powder into a bowl and mix in the ground almonds and sea salt. Fold into the chocolate mixture, then place on a floured tray (sheet), cover and leave to rest for at least 2 hours in the fridge.

2 Preheat the oven to 150°C (300°F/Gas 2). Roll the dough out to 1.5cm (¾ inch) thick on a lightly floured surface and cut out twelve 6cm (2½ inch) diameter circles. Place these inside twelve 6cm (2½ inch) tartlet rings standing on a baking tray (sheet) (or bake in batches if you do not have this many). Paint with egg wash and score with a fork in the traditional crossed pattern. Bake in the oven for 25–30 minutes until golden. Remove from the oven, carefully remove the metal rings and return to the oven for a further 10 minutes. Leave to cool.

CHOCOLATE CHIP COOKIES

Everyone loves a cookie, and these are a grown-up version of a classic.

Makes about 25 cookies

175g (6oz/generous 1 cup) plain (all-purpose) flour
1.5g (¼ tsp) baking powder
A pinch of salt
115g (4oz/1 stick plus 1 tbsp) unsalted butter, cut into cubes and softened
100g (3½oz/½ cup) light soft brown sugar
75g (2½oz/⅓ cup) caster (superfine) sugar
50g (1¾oz) whole eggs (about 1 egg)
30g (1oz) hazelnuts, roughly chopped and lightly roasted
85g (3oz/generous ¾ cup) walnuts, roughly chopped
200g (7oz) fine dark (bittersweet) chocolate (70% cocoa solids), finely chopped

1 Preheat the oven to 180°C (350°F/Gas 4). Line a baking tray (sheet) with a non-stick baking mat.

2 Sift the flour, baking powder and salt into a bowl. Put the butter and sugars in a bowl and cream together until light and fluffy. Gradually beat in the eggs until fully incorporated.

3 Mix in the flour, nuts and chocolate and spoon 3.5cm (1½ inch) discs onto the baking tray (sheet), keeping them well spaced apart to allow for spreading. (You may need to bake in batches, unless you have 2–3 baking trays/sheets.) Bake in the preheated oven for 20–25 minutes until golden brown. Leave to cool.

CHOCOLATE BISCUITS WITH COCOA NIBS

The cocoa nibs in this recipe act as the chocolate. They add a pleasant crunch as well as an element of acidic fruitiness.

Makes about 25 biscuits

125g (4½oz/1¼ sticks) unsalted butter, cut into cubes and softened
125g (4½oz/generous ½ cup) caster (superfine) sugar
¼ vanilla pod (bean), split lengthways
20ml (1½ tbsp) whipping (pouring) cream
125g (4½oz/generous ¾ cup) plain (all-purpose) flour
5g (1 tsp) baking powder
125g (4½oz/1⅔ cups) ground almonds
50g (1¾oz) cocoa nibs
Granulated (white) sugar, to sprinkle

1 Put the butter and sugar in a bowl and cream together until light and fluffy. Scrape in the seeds from the split vanilla pod (bean) along with the cream and mix well. Sift the flour and baking powder into a bowl, then mix in the ground almonds and cocoa nibs. Fold into the creamed butter mixture, place in a floured baking tray (sheet), wrap in cling film (plastic wrap) and leave to chill for at least 1 hour in the fridge.

2 Preheat the oven to 180°C (350°F/Gas 4). Roll the dough out to a thickness of 4mm (⅛ inch), cut into 5cm (2 inch) squares and place onto baking trays (sheets) lined with non-stick baking mats, leaving a 3cm (1 inch) gap between each square. Bake in the preheated oven for 12–15 minutes until light golden in colour. Lightly sprinkle with granulated sugar and leave to cool.

CHOCOLATE SABLÉS

A delicate, crumbly biscuit meaning 'sand' in French, originating from Normandy. Delicious with a mug of hot chocolate.

Makes about 25 sablés

150g (5½oz/1 cup) plain (all-purpose) flour
20g (¾oz/1 tbsp) cocoa powder
125g (4½oz/1¼ sticks) unsalted butter, cut into cubes and softened
75g (2½oz/½ cup) icing (powdered/pure) sugar
10g (¼oz) egg yolks (about ½ an egg)
Egg whites, for brushing
Granulated (white) sugar, for rolling

1 Preheat the oven to 160°C (325°F/Gas 3).

2 Sift the flour and cocoa powder into a bowl. Beat together the butter and sugar in a separate bowl until light in colour, about 2–3 minutes. Gradually add the egg yolks.

3 Add the dry ingredients and mix until it comes together as a dough.

4 Turn the dough out onto a lightly floured tray (sheet) or dish, cover with cling film (plastic wrap) and chill for 30 minutes in the fridge.

5 Roll the dough into a long sausage shape. Brush with egg white and then roll in the sugar. Cut into 1.5cm (¾ inch) slices and place on a non-stick baking tray (sheet).

6 Bake in the preheated oven for about 15–20 minutes. Leave to cool.

HOLLANDAISE BISCUITS

Although time consuming, these biscuits are fun to make, stunning to look at and delicious to eat when made well.

Makes about 25 biscuits

For the vanilla dough	For the chocolate dough
250g (9oz/1⅔ cups) plain (all-purpose) flour	140g (5oz/scant 1 cup) plain (all-purpose) flour
150g (5½oz/1½ sticks) unsalted butter, cut into cubes and softened	15g (½oz) cocoa powder
75g (2½oz/½ cup) icing (powdered/pure) sugar	90g (3oz/7 tbsp) unsalted butter, softened
¼ vanilla pod (bean), split lengthways	45g (1½oz/⅓ cup) icing (powdered/pure) sugar
25g (scant 1oz) egg yolk (about 1 egg)	15g (½oz) egg yolk (about 1 egg)
	Egg white

1 To make the vanilla dough, sift the flour into a bowl. Put the butter and sugar in a bowl, scrape in the seeds from the split vanilla pod (bean) and cream together until light and fluffy. Mix in the egg yolk and beat until smooth. Add the flour and mix to form a homogenous mass. Wrap in cling film (plastic wrap) and rest for at least 1 hour in the fridge.

2 To make the chocolate dough, sift the flour and cocoa powder into a bowl. Put the butter and sugar in a bowl and cream together until light and fluffy. Mix in the egg yolk and beat until smooth. Add the flour and cocoa power and mix to form a dough. Wrap in cling film (plastic wrap) and chill for at least 1 hour in the fridge.

 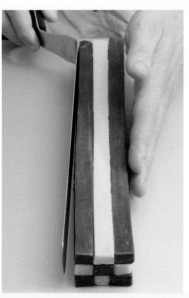  

3 To assemble, set aside one quarter of the vanilla dough. Roll out the remaining vanilla dough and all of the chocolate dough to 1cm (½ inch) thick and cut into 1cm (½ inch) wide strips. Carefully place a strip of the chocolate dough in front of you on the work surface. Lightly brush with the egg white and place a strip of the vanilla dough alongside it. Lightly brush with the egg white again and place a strip of the chocolate dough against the vanilla strip.

4 Repeat with two more layers on top, alternating the flavours in a checkerboard fashion until you have a block of dough, three strips high and three strips wide.

5 Roll out the remaining vanilla dough on a lightly floured surface to 3mm (⅛ inch) thick and about 12.5cm (5 inch) wide. Trim to neaten. Place this on top along the edge of the dough rectangle and wrap it around the checkerboard filling, joining neatly. Trim to neaten. Transfer to a baking tray (sheet) lined with silicone (baking) paper, loosely wrap in cling film (plastic wrap) and chill for 1 hour in the fridge. Preheat the oven to 180°C (350°F/Gas 4).

6 Cut the log into slices 1cm (½ inch) thick, place on a baking tray (sheet) lined with a non-stick baking mat and bake in the oven for 18–20 minutes until lightly golden.

PATISSERIE

The inspiration behind the modern patissier is Gaston Lenôtre. Known by the French as the 'gentleman pâtissier', he is widely credited with rejuvenating the world of patisserie in the 1960s by using less flour and sugar, opting instead for lightened mousses and taking advantage of technical innovations such as flash-freezing and gelatine. In the words of Pierre Hermé, Lenôtre 'dusted, lightened and modernized the heavy pastries of the 1950s'.

In the 1970s, nouvelle cuisine demanded a return to simple preparations and the freshest ingredients, and Lenôtre was frequently reported alongside the movement leaders (though his creations were certainly not simple). For me, he is someone who from humble beginnings has achieved extraordinary things, creating one of the first culinary brands and going on to train and inspire a whole generation of patissiers, including myself. In my younger days, I would take a night bus to Paris, just to look in shop windows such as his.

Our patisserie is based on modernizing classics, which traditionally have many components and are built in a structured and layered way. We have made the quantities for different elements smaller so that the recipes can be emulated in the home kitchen. However, always consider what I would do in my kitchen – if I have any leftover sponge I will freeze it to use another time. Raw pastry dough can be frozen, syrups and compotes can be stored in sealed containers in the fridge and macaroons can be frozen after being baked. It is important that any mousses are made as close to the assembly of the final patisserie as possible to avoid them setting prematurely.

DECORATING WITH CHOCOLATE

Using tempered chocolate, you can use various techniques to create delicate and attractive decorations for your patisserie. When you have created a piece of intricate patisserie, a special decoration, like the ones on the following pages, can allow them to look even more special and eye-catching.

1

2

3

Chocolate balls

1 Clean and polish a plastic sphere mould *(see Directory, page 224).* Using a ladle, fill the cavities up to the rim with tempered chocolate, scraping off any excess. Tap the sides of the mould with the scraper to remove the air bubbles.

2 Turn the mould upside down over the bain-marie (water bath) of tempered chocolate and tap with the scraper again to remove any further excess chocolate.

3 Place the mould upside down on a baking tray (sheet) lined with a non-stick baking mat (or a flat baking tray (sheet) lined with silicone (baking) paper) and leave it to set for about 2 hours in a cool, dry area, or until the chocolate has come away from the mould.

4 Twist the mould like an ice-cube tray to loosen the chocolate spheres, then turn it upside down onto a clean surface.

5 Warm a saucepan on the stove and turn it over. Carefully place two of the chocolate spheres onto the pan bottom for a second, then stick the two spheres together to make a ball. Place the balls back in the mould to prevent them moving. Leave to fully set.

Chocolate twists

1 Cut out triangles from a sheet of acetate. Spread each triangle with a thin layer of chocolate using a palette knife. Leave to almost set.

2 Carefully using the tip of a small knife, lift the triangle from the thin layer of chocolate. Place it in a curved shape mould *(see Directory, page 224)* at an angle and leave to set for at least 2 hours in a cool, dry area. It will contract and form a more pronounced twist as it sets. Remove the acetate strip when ready to use.

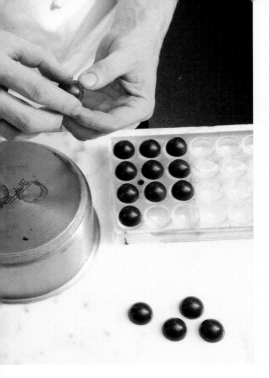

Chocolate copeaux

1 Spread a thin layer of tempered chocolate onto a marble or granite slab using a stepped palette knife and leave it to almost set .

2 Using a metal scraper, push at an angle against the layer of chocolate to create thin cigar shapes (copeaux) – a short, sharp movement to the side will cause the copeaux to stay on the marble.

3 Leave the copeaux to set on the surface for a few minutes and then remove with the metal scraper.

Note:
For all decorations the chocolate must be tempered *(see pages 18–19).*

COMBING & PIPING
TECHNIQUES

Note:
Each of these
decorations requires
an 18 × 40cm (7 × 16
inch) strip of acetate.

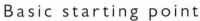

Basic starting point

Chocolate hoops

Carefully lift the chocolate-coated
acetate from the work surface and
wrap it around a plastic tube, with
the chocolate against the tube, and
leave to set for at least 2 hours in
a cool, dry area. Carefully remove
the chocolate from the plastic tube
(as long as you have used a plastic
surface, set chocolate will always
come away easily) and separate
the thin strips to make several thin
chocolate hoops.

Spoon a small amount of tempered chocolate onto an acetate strip and, using a small stepped palette knife, spread the chocolate into a thin layer. Scrape with a comb scraper from left to right along the length of the acetate and leave to almost set.

Chocolate curls

Carefully lift the chocolate-coated acetate from the work surface and curl it round on itself to create a spiral. Place it in a curved tray to help retain the curl while it sets completely. Leave it to set for at least 2 hours in a cool, dry area. Separate the thin strips to make several thin chocolate curls.

Chocolate waves

Place another strip of acetate on top of the chocolate and then carefully position it between two sheets of corrugated plastic. Press down gently and leave to set for at least 2 hours in a cool, dry area. Carefully remove the plastic and the acetate from the chocolate when ready to use and separate the thin strips to make several thin chocolate waves.

Piped curls

Make a small piping (pastry) bag with silicone (baking) paper and half fill with tempered chocolate (make sure the hole is small, less than 1mm). Pipe thin lines of chocolate along the acetate and leave to almost set. Carefully lift the chocolate-coated acetate and curl it round on itself to create a spiral. Place it in a curved tray and leave to set for at least 2 hours in a cool, dry area. Remove the acetate when ready to use.

FLAT SHEET TECHNIQUES

1 Spoon some tempered chocolate onto an acetate sheet (you can personalize your decorations using decorated acetate or simply use plain sheets) and spread it out to a thin layer. Leave to almost set in a cool, dry area.

2 To make squares, set some metal wheels to your desired size and run them over the chocolate to cut out square shapes. Or, use a small, sharp knife to score the squares.

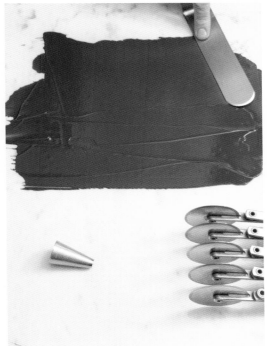

1

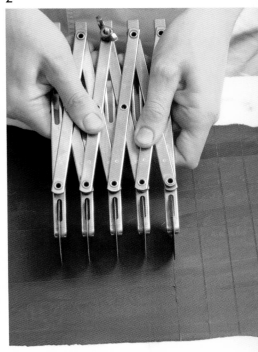

2

3

4

5

3 To cut out holes from the squares, cut the centre of each square out using the top of a small metal piping nozzle (tip).

4 Put another sheet of acetate on top of the scored chocolate and then place it between two Perspex or flat baking trays (sheets). Their weight prevents the chocolate curling as it sets. Leave to fully set for at least 2 hours in a cool, dry area.

5 Peel away the acetate sheets and separate the squares when ready to use. You can use the same method to create different shape decorations – discs for Florentines (*see page 100*) or rectangles for Milionaire's Shortbread (*see page 112*) for example.

PRALINE PASTE

Praline dates back to the 1730s in France. It is traditionally made with almonds, but now various nuts including hazelnuts and walnuts are used. We use Piedmont hazelnuts and Avola almonds for our praline, two of the finest variety of nuts you can buy – smooth and rich with no bitterness.

Praline is widely used by patissiers and chocolatiers in recipes to make patisserie, chocolates, cakes, ice cream and desserts. One of my favourite patisseries, Paris Brest (see page 187) is flavoured with praline.

Makes about 500g (1lb)

150g (5½oz/1 cup) hazelnuts
150g (5½oz/¾ cup) almonds
250g (9oz/generous 1 cup) caster (superfine) sugar
10ml (¾ tbsp) hazelnut oil

1

2

3

1 Preheat the oven to 200°C (400°F/Gas 6) and spread the nuts out on a non-stick baking tray (sheet). Roast in the oven for 8–10 minutes until lightly golden and then transfer to a heavy-based saucepan.

2 Cook over a medium heat while gradually adding the sugar and stirring continuously.

3 Continue to cook and stir until the sugar turns an amber caramel, about 15–18 minutes.

4 Pour the caramelized nuts onto a baking tray lined with a non-stick baking mat and leave to cool.

5 When the nuts have cooled, break up the praline and transfer it to a good food processor or blender (we use a Thermomix, see page 224).

6 Add the hazelnut oil and blitz until you have a smooth paste. Store in an airtight container for up to 1 month.

CHOCOLATE MOUSSE

Chocolate mousse features in the majority of our patisserie recipes as it is a light way of adding rich chocolate flavour, and mastering a good chocolate mousse is essential to mastering patisserie. The anglaise method works better for smaller batches, and although both have similar results, the sabayon method will give a slightly lighter result.

Makes 10–12 portions

150ml (5fl oz/⅔ cup) milk
550ml (17fl oz/2¼ cups) whipping
  (pouring) cream (30% butter fat)
1 vanilla pod (bean), split lengthways

60g (2oz) egg yolks (about 3 eggs)
30g (1oz) caster (superfine) sugar
320g (11oz) fine dark (bittersweet) chocolate
  (66% cocoa solids), finely chopped

1

2

3

Anglaise method

1 Put the milk, 150ml (5fl oz/ ⅔ cup) of the cream and the scraped seeds and split vanilla pod (bean) in a saucepan. Bring to the boil. Meanwhile, whisk the egg yolks and sugar together in a large mixing bowl until it turns light in colour, about 2–3 minutes.

2 When the milk has boiled, pour half of it onto the egg yolk and sugar mixture and mix thoroughly.

3 Pour this mix back into the pan and cook over a low heat, stirring continuously, until the mixture is thick enough to coat the back of a spoon.

4 Take off the heat and pass through a fine sieve (strainer) onto the chopped chocolate in a mixing bowl.

5 Using a spatula, mix until smooth and emulsified and then leave to cool.

6 Place the remaining whipping cream into a mixing bowl and whisk until soft peaks form. Alternatively, whisk in an electric mixer fitted with the whisk attachment.

7 Carefully fold the whipped cream into the chocolate mixture and use immediately.

4   5   7

Sabayon method

300g (10oz) fine dark (bittersweet)
chocolate (63% cocoa solids), finely
chopped

140g (5oz) egg yolks

80g (3oz/⅓ cup) caster
(superfine) sugar

40ml (1½fl oz/2 tbsp) water

380ml (13fl oz/1½ cups) whipping
(pouring) cream (30% butter fat)

1 Melt the chocolate in a bain-marie
(water bath) until it reaches 45°C
(113°F). Whisk the egg yolks in an
electric mixer fitted with the whisk
attachment. Meanwhile, put the sugar
and water in a saucepan and bring to
the boil. Cook until it reaches 121°C
(250°F) and then slowly pour the
sugar syrup over the egg yolks and
continue to whisk to a full sabayon
(until the mix reaches the ribbon stage,

becoming thick and pale). Continue
to whisk the mixture until it is cool.

2 In a separate bowl, whisk the
cream until it reaches the ribbon
stage (see page 218) and then
fold the cream into the sabayon.
Carefully fold one-third of the
mixture into the melted chocolate
and then fold in the remainder.
Use immediately.

CHOCOLATE RUM BABA

This is a very simple dessert – our version is soaked in chocolate syrup to make it a little richer and give it more depth.

Makes 18

200ml (7fl oz/generous ¾ cup) dark rum, for drizzling

For the rum-soaked raisins
250g (9oz/1½ cups) raisins, washed and drained
150ml (5fl oz/⅔ cup) dark rum

For the baba dough
60ml (2fl oz/¼ cup) milk
20g (¾oz) fresh yeast
230g (8oz/1½ cups) plain flour, sifted
20g (¾oz) caster (superfine) sugar
1g (a pinch) salt
150g (5½oz) whole eggs (about 3 eggs)
100g (3½oz/1 stick) unsalted butter, softened, plus extra for greasing

For the chocolate syrup
450ml (15fl oz/1¾ cups) water
375g (13oz/1⅔ cups) caster (superfine) sugar
50g (1¾oz/½ cup) cocoa powder
50g (1¾oz) fine dark (bittersweet) chocolate (70% cocoa solids), roughly chopped

For the crème Chantilly
120ml (4fl oz/½ cup) whipping (pouring) cream (30% butter fat)
120ml (4fl oz/½ cup) double (heavy) cream
½ vanilla pod, split lengthways
15g (½oz) caster (superfine) sugar

Notes:
• Make the rum-soaked raisins in advance and store in an airtight container until needed.
• You could make less than 18 by assembling the components as required and freezing any leftover baba sponges.
• You will need 18 canelle or dariole moulds *(see page 224)*.

The day before, make the rum-soaked raisins:

1 Put the raisins in an airtight container and add the rum. Seal and leave to marinate overnight.

The next day, make the babas:

2 Put the milk in a saucepan and heat gently to a temperature of about 30°C (86°F) – be careful not to overheat or you will kill the yeast. Pour the milk into a mixing bowl and add in the yeast; stir until it's dissolved. Mix in 30g (1oz) of the sifted flour, cover with a cloth and leave in a warm place for about 20 minutes until doubled in size (this is the sponge ferment).

3 Put the remaining flour, sugar and salt in the bowl of an electric mixer and combine. Add the eggs and the sponge ferment and mix on a moderate speed with a dough hook until the dough comes away from the side of the bowl, about 10 minutes. Alternatively, knead by hand in a large mixing bowl. Gradually mix in the butter until fully incorporated. Cover with a cloth and leave to prove in a warm area until it has doubled in size, about 30–45 minutes.

4 Lightly grease the moulds (see Note opposite). Knock back the dough and transfer to a piping (pastry) bag, snip a small hole in the end and pipe into the greased moulds so that they are just over half full. Leave to prove until the top of the dough rises just above the level of the mould, about 20–30 minutes. Meanwhile, preheat the oven to 200°C (400°F/Gas 6).

5 Bake the moulds in the oven for 25 minutes, then lower the oven temperature to 160° (325°F/Gas 3) to dry out for a further 12–15 minutes. Remove from the moulds and freeze any you don't want to use straightaway once cooled.

To assemble & finish:

6 Make the chocolate syrup. Boil together the water and sugar in a saucepan. Add the cocoa powder, re-boil and cook over a low heat for a further 2 minutes. Pass through a fine sieve (strainer) over a bowl containing the chopped chocolate and mix until fully combined.

7 Pour the syrup into a shallow tray and add in the babas. Use a spoon to pour syrup over the tops so that the cakes are completely coated. Once they are fully soaked, carefully lift them out, place on a serving dish and leave to cool. Pour 1 tablespoon of dark rum over each baba.

8 To make the crème Chantilly, whisk both creams, the vanilla seeds from the pod (bean) and the sugar together until soft peaks form and spoon into a piping (pastry) bag ready for piping.

9 Place a spoonful of the rum-soaked sultanas onto a serving dish. Carefully, using a large spoon, place a baba on top of the sultanas. Pipe a bulb of the crème Chantilly by the side of the baba and repeat with the remaining babas.

CHOCOLATE TARTS

The very first job I had was in a small restaurant in Scotland, under the guidance of Scott Lyall. He is fantastic at training young chefs, many of whom have gone on to have great careers. Scott would be very influenced by current French trends, researching, tasting and then developing his own recipes. He was a great influence on my early development and I really enjoyed my time there when I would make these tarts with him. This is also a favourite of chocolate connoisseur Sara Jayne Stanes.

Makes 15–16 tarts

1 quantity Hazelnut & Almond Pastry (*see page 190*), but replace the ground hazelnuts with another 50g (1¾oz/⅔ cup) ground almonds

⅔ quantity Basic Ganache (*see pages 22–23*)

1 quantity Crème Chantilly (*see page 162*)

Chocolate decorations (*see pages 152–157*) and edible gold leaf, to finish

For the soft chocolate sponge

85g (3oz) fine dark (bittersweet) chocolate (63% cocoa solids), chopped

40g (1½oz/3 tbsp) unsalted butter, softened

25g (scant 1oz) egg yolks (about 1 egg)

80g (2¾oz) egg whites (about 3 eggs)

40g (1½oz/scant ¼ cup) caster (superfine) sugar

For the chocolate glasage

130ml (4½fl oz/½ cup) whipping (pouring) cream)

25g (scant 1oz) caster (superfine) sugar

20g (scant 1oz) liquid glucose

125g (4½oz) fine dark (bittersweet) chocolate (63% cocoa solids), chopped

Notes:
- You will need 15–16 tartlet tins measuring 7cm (2¾ inches) in diameter and 3cm (1½ inches) deep (*see page 224*).
- The pastry dough and the cooked sponge can be made in advance, wrapped well and frozen.

First, prepare & chill the pastry:

1 Follow the instructions in step 1 on page 190, but use the pastry to line 15–16 tartlet tins, trim and rest for at least 30 minutes in the fridge.

Meanwhile, bake the sponge:

2 Preheat the oven to 160°C (325°F/Gas 3). Melt the chocolate over a bain-marie (water bath) to 45°C (113°F). Take off the heat, add the softened butter and stir until fully combined. Add the egg yolks and mix until fully incorporated.

3 In a mixing bowl, slowly whisk the egg whites, gradually adding the sugar and increasing the speed. Continue to whisk to a soft peak meringue (see page 218). Alternatively, whisk in an elextric mixer fitted with the whisk attachment. Add one-third of the meringue to the chocolate mixture and mix until smooth. Carefully fold in the remaining meringue.

4 Spoon the sponge mixture into a piping (pastry) bag fitted with a 12mm (½ inch) plain nozzle (tip) and pipe 3.5cm (1½ inch) discs onto a non-stick baking mat. Bake in the oven for 12–15 minutes, then transfer to a wire rack to cool completely.

Next, cook the pastry:

5 Increase the oven temperature to 180°C (350°F/Gas 4). Using silicone (baking) paper, line the pastry cases and fill with baking beans. Bake in the oven for 15 minutes. Remove the silicone (baking) paper and baking beans, then return to the oven and continue to bake for a further 10–12 minutes until golden brown. Cool on a wire rack and remove the casees from the moulds.

Make the glasage:

6 Put the cream, sugar and liquid glucose in a saucepan and bring to the boil. Gradually add the cream to the chopped chocolate, mixing continuously to form an emulsion and use immediately.

To assemble & finish:

7 Pour the basic ganache using a jug into the base of each tartlet case until one-third full. Place a chocolate sponge disc on top of this. Pour more ganache into the tart until it reaches the top of the tart. Transfer to the fridge to set for about 20 minutes.

8 Carefully spoon a thin layer of the chocolate glasage on top of the tart and leave to set. Make the crème chantilly and shape into quenelles. Place the quenelles on top of the tart and decorate with chocolate decorations and edible gold leaf.

CLASSIC MILLE FEUILLE

This is my take on a version I used to make with Pierre Koffmann at La Tante Claire.

Makes 12 portions

1 quantity **Pastry Cream** (see Chocolate Pastry Cream, *page 187*), made without the cocoa powder and chocolate and 80g (2¾oz) plain (all-purpose) flour
½ quantity **Crème Chantilly** (see *page 162*)
Chocolate decorations (see *pages 152–157*)

For the rough puff pastry
250g (9oz/1⅔ cups) soft flour
250g (9oz/1⅔ cups) strong flour
8g (¼oz/1½ tsp) salt
500g (1lb 2oz/5 sticks) unsalted butter
225ml (7½fl oz/scant 1 cup) cold water
Icing sugar, to dust

For the chocolate diplomat cream
250ml (9fl oz/1 cup) milk
½ vanilla pod (bean), split lengthways
60g (2oz) egg yolks (about 3 eggs)
75g (2½oz/⅓ cup) caster (superfine) sugar
20g (¾oz) plain (all-purpose) flour, sifted
20g (¾oz/1 tbsp) cocoa powder
30g (1oz) fine dark (bittersweet) chocolate (70% cocoa solids), chopped
150ml (5fl oz/⅔ cup) double (heavy) cream (36% butter fat)

For the caramelized honey apples
125g (4½oz/generous ½ cup) caster (superfine) sugar
50g (1¾oz) runny honey
3 apples, peeled, cored and each apple cut into 12 wedges
15ml (1 tbsp) Sauternes or sweet wine

First, prepare the puff pastry:

1 Sift the flours and salt onto a clean work surface and add the cubed butter into the centre of the flour. Using your fingertips, work the ingredients together until the mixture becomes grainy. Make a well in the centre and pour in two-thirds of the cold water, mixing until the dough starts to come

together. Add the remaining water and form the dough into a homogenous mass that contains flakes of butter – do not knead. Wrap in cling film (plastic wrap) and chill for 20 minutes. On a lightly floured surface, roll out the dough to a 40 × 20cm (16 × 8 inch) rectangle. Fold one short side over so that the edge lies two-thirds of the way across the rectangle and then fold the other short side over this to make three layers. This is the first turn. Rotate the dough 90 degrees and roll out again, repeat the folding process (this is your second turn). Place on a lightly floured tray (sheet), cover with cling film (plastic wrap) and chill for at least 30 minutes. Rotate the dough 90 degrees and then repeat the two turns as described above. Leave to chill for 1 hour.

Meanwhile, make the diplomat cream, the apples & cook the pastry:

2 For the cream, put the milk and vanilla pod (bean) in a pan and heat gently, slowly bringing to the boil. In a mixing bowl, whisk together the egg yolks and the sugar until light in colour, about 2–3 minutes. Add the flour and cocoa and whisk again until smooth. Pour half of the boiled milk into the bowl and whisk until there are no lumps. Pass through a fine sieve (strainer), then return to the milk in the pan. Continuously whisk until it comes to the boil and then reduce the temperature to a simmer. Continue to stir and cook for about 5 minutes. Take off the heat, add in the chocolate and stir until it has melted. Pour the cream into a shallow tray, wrap with cling film (plastic wrap) and cool rapidly.

3 Whip the double (heavy) cream in a large bowl to a soft peak. In a separate bowl, beat the chocolate cream until smooth, and then fold in the whipped cream.

4 For the apples, heat a heavy-based pan, add one-third of the sugar and cook to a caramel. Gradually add the remaining sugar. Once an amber caramel forms, add the honey and cook for 2 minutes. Add the apples and cook over a low heat for 5–8 minutes. The caramel will penetrate the apples leaving them golden. Take the pan off the heat, add the wine and leave the apples to cool in the caramel.

5 On a lightly floured surface cut the dough in half and roll out to 5mm (¼ inch) thick. Place the pastry onto a baking tray (sheet) lined with a non-stick baking mat. Repeat with the remaining pastry and a second baking tray (sheet). Chill for 30 minutes. Preheat the oven to 200°C (400°F/Gas 6). Prick the pastry with a fork. Dust liberally with icing sugar and bake for 25–30 minutes until the pastry has risen and is golden brown. Leave to cool on a wire rack.

To assemble & finish:

6 Using a serrated knife, cut the puff pastry into 4 × 10cm (1½ × 4 inch) rectangles – you will need a total of 36 rectangles. Spoon the pastry cream into a piping (pastry) bag fitted with a 10mm (½ inch) nozzle (tip) and pipe rows across the base layer of pastry. Drain the apples, place 6 wedges on the cream and top with a second pastry layer. Spoon the chocolate diplomat cream into a piping (pastry) bag fitted with a 12mm (½ inch) nozzle (tip) and pipe bulbs across the pastry. Top with the final pastry layer. Spoon the crème Chantilly into a piping (pastry) bag fitted with a 10mm (½ inch) fluted nozzle (tip) and pipe a bulb on top and decorate with chocolate decorations.

CHOCOLATE MONT BLANC

This Mont Blanc patisserie takes its name from the snow-capped mountains. Suzue is the expert within the business for making the best ones.

Makes 15

1 quantity **Chocolate Diplomat Cream**
(*see page 166*)

For the chestnut mousse
7g (1 generous tsp) leaf gelatine
65g (2¼oz/generous ¼ cup) caster
  (superfine) sugar
65ml (2fl oz/¼ cup) water
175g (6oz) unsweetened chestnut purée
30ml (1fl oz/2 tbsp) dark rum
300ml (10fl oz/1¼ cups) double
  (heavy) cream (36% butter fat)

For the chocolate macaroons
(*makes about 35 small macaroons*)
20g (¾oz/1 tbsp) cocoa powder, sifted
100g (3½oz/1¼ cups) ground almonds
100g (3½oz) egg whites (about 3½ eggs)
100g (3½oz/scant ½ cup) caster
  (superfine) sugar

For the chestnut & rum buttercream
115g (4oz/1 stick plus 1 tbsp) unsalted
  butter, softened
275g (9½oz) chestnut purée
20ml (1 tbsp) dark rum
45g (1½oz) egg whites (about 1½ eggs)
90g (3oz/generous ⅓ cup) caster
  (superfine) sugar

To finish
Cocoa powder
Vacuum-packed candied chestnuts,
  quartered
½ quantity **Crème Chantilly** (*see page 162*)
Chocolate Copeaux (*see page 153*)

First, make the chestnut mousse:

1 Put the gelatine in enough cold water to cover it, soak for a few minutes until soft and then gently squeeze off any excess water. Put the sugar, water and chestnut purée in a pan and bring to the boil. Add the gelatine and stir to dissolve. Take off the heat and blitz the mixture with a hand-held blender and then pass through a sieve (strainer) into a bowl. Leave to cool. Then mix in the dark rum. In a separate bowl, whip the cream until soft peaks form and then fold this into the chestnut mixture. Transfer to an airtight container and keep in the fridge until needed. Leave to set for 2–3 hours in the fridge.

Second, make the macaroons:

2 Preheat the oven to 140°C (275°F/ Gas 1) and line a baking tray (sheet) with a non-stick baking mat. Mix the cocoa powder and ground almonds in a bowl. In a separate bowl, slowly whisk the egg whites by hand, gradually adding the sugar and increasing the speed. Continue whisking to a firm meringue. Alternatively, whisk the egg whites in an electric mixer fitted with the whisk attachment.

3 Fold the cocoa powder and almond mixture into the meringue. Spoon the mixture into a piping (pastry) bag fitted with a 14mm (¾ inch) plain nozzle (tip) and pipe out 5cm (2 inch) discs onto the prepared tray (sheet) leaving a 3.5cm (1½ inch) gap between each. Bake in the oven for 35–40 minutes. Remove and leave to cool on a wire rack.

Next, make the buttercream:

4 In a mixing bowl, cream the butter and gradually add the chestnut purée. Beat until smooth and then stir in the rum. Meanwhile, in a separate mixing bowl, whisk the egg whites and sugar over a bain-marie (water bath) until the mixture reaches 60°C (140°F). Take off the heat and continue to whisk until soft peaks form and the mixture cools. Mix the meringue into the creamed butter mixture.

Finally, to assemble & finish:

5 Place a macaroon on a small serving dish. Spoon the buttercream into a piping (pastry) bag fitted with a 15mm (¾ inch) plain nozzle (tip) and pipe a 4cm (1½ inch) bulb on top. Chill for 30 minutes. Using a palette knife, spread a layer of the chocolate diplomat cream evenly around the chestnut and rum buttercream so that it is completely covered.

6 Spoon the mousse into a piping (pastry) bag fitted with a Mont Blanc nozzle (tip) and pipe layers of the mousse on top by rotating the bag over and across the buttercream, building up three layers in total. Lightly dust with cocoa powder. Pipe a bulb of crème Chantilly on top and decorate with a chopped candied chestnut and a chocolate copeaux. Repeat with the remaining ingredients to make 15 Mont Blancs in total.

> **Notes:**
> • The macaroons and buttercream can both be made in advance and frozen.

CHOCOLATE & APRICOT ROULADE

Although a traditional dish here, these are known as roll cakes in Japan, where they are becoming innovative and incredibly popular.

Makes 12–14 slices

Chocolate decorations *(see pages 152–157)* and edible gold leaf, to finish

For the chocolate roulade sponge
175g (6oz) egg whites (about 5½ eggs)
175g (6oz/¾ cup) caster (superfine) sugar
210g (7½oz) egg yolks (about 10½ eggs)
150g (5½oz/1 cup) plain (all-purpose) flour, sifted
30g (1oz/¼ cup) cocoa powder, sifted

For the apricot ganache
500g (1lb 2oz) ready-made apricot purée *(OR see Blackcurrant Purée, page 124)*
100g (3½oz/scant ½ cup) caster (superfine) sugar
25ml (scant 1fl oz) lemon juice
300g (10oz) fine dark (bittersweet) chocolate (63% cocoa solids), finely chopped

For the apricot mousse
210g (7½oz) apricot purée *(see Blackcurrant Purée, page 124)*
50g (1¾oz/¼ cup) caster (superfine) sugar
7g (1 generous tsp) leaf gelatine
300ml (½ pint/1¼ cups) whipping (pouring) cream (30% butter fat)

> **Notes:**
> • The roulade sponge could be made in advance and frozen.

First, make the roulade sponge:

1 Preheat the oven to 180°C (350°F/Gas 4). In a mixing bowl, slowly whisk the egg whites, gradually adding the sugar and increasing the speed. Continue to whisk to a soft peak meringue. Alternatively, whisk the egg whites in an electric mixer fitted with the whisk attachment. Gradually whisk in the egg yolks and then carefully fold in the sifted flour and cocoa powder.

2 Spread the sponge mixture carefully between two 25.5 × 30cm (10 × 12 inch) deep-sided baking trays (sheets) lined with non-stick baking mats. Bake in the preheated oven for 18–20 minutes until golden and the top of the sponge springs back when pressed. Remove from the oven, place a sheet of silicone (baking) paper on top of each one and leave to cool on a wire rack.

Meanwhile, make the apricot ganache:

3 Put the apricot purée and sugar in a saucepan and bring to the boil. Add the lemon juice and stir to combine. Cook over a low heat for 2–3 minutes. Pour the apricot mixture into a bowl containing the chopped chocolate. Using a spatula, mix until it forms an emulsion. Leave to cool and thicken in a cool, dry area.

Finally, make the apricot mousse:

4 Put the apricot purée and sugar in a saucepan and bring to the boil. Take off the heat. In a small bowl, soak the gelatine in enough cold water to just cover it, soak for a few minutes until soft and then gently squeeze off any excess water. Add the gelatine to the apricot purée and sugar, stir until it is dissolved and then leave to cool until it reaches about 40°C (104°F).

5 Put the cream in the bowl of an electric mixer fitted with the whisk attachment and whisk the cream until it forms soft peaks. Alternatively, whisk by hand in a mixing bowl. Fold the whipped cream into the apricot purée and leave to cool and thicken for about 10 minutes.

To assemble & finish:

6 Turn both sponges over onto the two sheets of silicone (baking) paper you topped them with on a flat surface and carefully peel away the baking mats.

7 Spread the cooled and thickened ganache evenly onto the sponges leaving a gap of 5cm (2 inches) along one of the long edges. Spread the apricot mousse on top of the ganache. Roll up the roulades starting with the long edge that is covered with ganache and mousse. Roll tightly with the help of the silicone paper to roll it over. When rolled up the roulades should sit on the edge of the sponge that contained no mousse or ganache. Leave in the fridge for at least 2 hours to firm up.

8 When ready to serve, remove from the fridge, trim the ends with a hot, dry knife and cut each roulade into 6–7 slices. Decorate with chocolate decorations and edible gold leaf.

CHOCOLATE FINANCIER with passion fruit curd

This was inspired by the style of cooking used during my time working for Raymond Blanc at Le Manoir aux Quat'Saisons.

Makes 15

Chocolate decorations (*see pages 152–157*) and edible gold leaf, to finish

For the passion fruit curd
1.5g (¼ tsp) leaf gelatine
100g (3½oz) ready-made passion fruit purée
200g (7oz) whole eggs (about 4 eggs)
90g (3oz/ generous ⅓ cup) caster (superfine) sugar
90g (3oz/7 tbsp) unsalted butter
2 passion fruits

For the chocolate financier
260g (9¼oz/2⅔ sticks) unsalted butter
20g (¾oz) fine dark (bittersweet) chocolate (66% cocoa solids), chopped
250g (9oz/generous 1½ cups) icing (powdered/pure) sugar, sifted
20g (¾oz/1 tbsp) cocoa powder
125g (4½oz/1⅓ cups) ground almonds
85g (3oz/generous ½ cup) plain (all-purpose) flour, sifted
240g (8½oz) egg whites (about 8 eggs)
25g (scant 1oz) orange marmalade

For the poached mango
150ml (5fl oz/⅔ cup) water
90g (3oz/generous ⅓ cup) caster (superfine) sugar
7g (1 tsp) fresh root ginger, grated
1 large mango (about 150g/5½oz)
Zest and juice of 1 lime

For the passion fruit glaze
250g (9oz) ready-made passion fruit purée
20g (¾oz) caster (superfine) sugar
3g (½ tsp) leaf gelatine
½ vanilla pod (bean), split lengthways

For the rum syrup
180ml (6fl oz/¾ cup) water
170g (6oz/¾ cup) caster (superfine) sugar
150ml (5fl oz/⅔ cup) dark rum
½ vanilla pod, split lengthways

First, make the passion fruit curd:

1 Place fifteen 4.5cm (1¾ inch) dome moulds onto a baking tray (sheet). Put the gelatine in a bowl with enough cold water to just cover it, soak for a few minutes until soft and then squeeze off any excess water. Put the passion fruit purée in a saucepan and bring to the boil. Meanwhile, in a large mixing bowl, whisk the whole eggs and sugar together until the mixture becomes light in colour. Add half of the passion fruit purée and mix until smooth. Pass through a fine sieve (strainer) into a mixing bowl and then combine with the purée in the saucepan. Continue to cook over a low heat for a further 3–4 minutes. Take off the heat, mix in the butter, add the gelatine and stir to dissolve. Cut each passion fruit in half and add the seeds to the saucepan. Pour the curd into the prepared moulds and transfer to the freezer for about 2–3 hours or until frozen.

Second, make the chocolate financier:

2 Preheat the oven to 180°C (350°F/ Gas 4). Make a beurre noisette by cooking the butter in a pan until it becomes nut brown, about 10 minutes. Leave to cool to 40°C (104°F). Melt the chopped chocolate over a bain-marie (water bath) to 45°C (113°F). Put the sugar, cocoa powder, ground almonds and flour into a bowl and mix the dry ingredients and egg whites. Add the butter and the melted chocolate and mix until smooth. Add the marmalade and stir to mix. Transfer the mixture to an airtight container and chill for 20 minutes. Spoon the mixture into a piping (pastry) bag, snip a small hole in the end and pipe into a 15-hole silicone financier mould. Bake for about 15–20 minutes, then leave to cool slightly.

Meanwhile, make the poached mango:

3 Put the water, sugar and grated ginger in a saucepan and bring to the boil. Meanwhile, wash, peel and stone the mangoes and cut into 1cm (½inch) cubes. Add the mango cubes and lime zest and juice to the saucepan and continue to cook for 2–3 minutes. Take off the heat and leave to cool. Use the poached mango once cooled or store in airtight container in the fridge until needed.

Next, make the glaze & rum syrup:

4 For the glaze, put the passion fruit purée in a saucepan. Scrape the vanilla seeds into the pan and drop in the empty pod. Bring to the boil and continue to cook until it has reduced by half and then add the sugar Put the gelatine in enough cold water to just cover it, soak for a few seconds until soft and then squeeze off any excess water. Add the gelatine to the saucepan and stir to dissolve. Pass through a fine sieve (strainer), then leave to cool.

5 For the syrup, Put the water, sugar and vanilla in a pan and bring to the boil. Take off the heat and leave to cool. Once cool, add the rum. Transfer to an airtight container and chill until needed.

To assemble & finish:

6 Trim the base of each financier and dip in the syrup. Place the poached mango in the cavities of the financiers. Gently melt the passion fruit glaze to about 40°C (104°F), then cool to 26–28°C (79–82°F). Dip the curd into the glaze while it is frozen and place on top of the mango. Chill for 30 minutes to allow the curd to defrost. Decorate with chocolate decorations and edible gold leaf.

ORANGE & CHOCOLATE SACHER

So named after its creator, Franz Sacher, this recipe was invented in 1832 when he was a young apprentice, and has become a well-known and popular dessert that you will find in most patisseries. It even has its own national day of recognition (December 5th) in Austria. There was a long-fought legal battle over the recipe of the official sacher tortes, which has always been a closely guarded secret. This is our tribute to it, with a few of our contemporary twists thrown in. This cake was originally served with a garnish of whipped cream and made using apricot marmalade. We have replaced the marmalade with an orange jam and ganache and used the cream to make a mousse layer.

Makes about 16 slices

1 quantity Chocolate Mousse – Anglaise Method (*see page 160*)

For the sacher sponge
50g (1¾oz/⅔ cup) ground almonds
50g (1¾oz/¼ cup) caster (superfine)sugar
75g (2½oz) egg whites (about 2½ eggs)
60g (2oz/generous ⅓ cup) icing (powdered/pure) sugar
40g (1½oz) whole eggs (about 1 egg)
50g (1¾oz) egg yolks (about 2½ eggs)
25g (scant 1oz) fine dark (bittersweet) chocolate (70% cocoa solids), finely chopped
25g (scant 1oz/2 tbsp) unsalted butter
25g (scant 1oz) plain (all-purpose) flour, sifted
15g (½oz/1 tbsp) cocoa powder, sifted

For the Alhambra sponge
100g (3½oz/1 stick) unsalted butter
25g (scant 1oz) plain (all-purpose) flour, sifted
25g (scant 1oz) cornflour (cornstarch)
30g (1oz/¼ cup) cocoa powder
200g (7oz) whole eggs (about 4 eggs)
50g (1¾oz) egg yolks (about 2½ eggs)
80g (3oz/generous ⅓ cup) caster (superfine) sugar

For the orange jam
Peeled rind of 2 oranges, pith removed
400g (14oz) orange flesh, outer pith removed (about 3–4 small oranges)
120ml (4fl oz/½ cup) orange juice
330g (11oz) jam sugar

For the Grand Marnier syrup
170g (6oz/¾ cup) caster (superfine) sugar
180ml (6fl oz/¾ cup) water
½ vanilla pod (bean), split lengthways
150ml (5fl oz/⅔ cup) Grand Marnier

For the orange ganache
75g (2½oz) fine dark (bittersweet) chocolate (65% cocoa solids), chopped
75g (2½oz) fine milk chocolate, finely chopped
200ml (7fl oz/generous ¾ cup) orange juice
20g (¾oz) caster (superfine) sugar
25g (scant 1oz) unsalted butter, cubed

For the orange & chocolate glaze
50g (1¾oz) fine dark (bittersweet) chocolate (70% cocoa solids), finely chopped
6g (1 tsp) leaf gelatine
500ml (16fl oz/2 cups) orange juice
½ vanilla pod (bean), split lengthways
40g (1½oz) caster (superfine) sugar

To finish
Chocolate decorations (*see pages 152–157*)
Edible gold leaf (optional)

Notes:
- You will need two 37 × 9 × 4cm (15 × 3½ × 1½ inch) mousse frames (*see page 224*).
- Both sponges can be made in advance and frozen.

First, make the sacher sponge:

1 Preheat the oven to 180°C (350°F/ Gas 4). Line a 25.5 × 30cm (10 × 12 inch) baking tray (sheet) with a non-stick baking mat. Beat together the ground almonds, caster (superfine) sugar and 20g (¾oz) of the egg whites in a bowl. Gradually mix in 30g (1oz) of the icing (powdered/pure) sugar until smooth, then slowly mix in the whole eggs and egg yolks and beat for 4–5 minutes until smooth and light. In a separate bowl, whisk the remaining egg whites and gradually add the remaining icing (powdered/pure) sugar. Whisk to a soft-peak meringue (*see page 218*).

2 Melt the chocolate over a bain-marie (water bath), then remove from the heat and add the unsalted butter. Mix until smooth, then add the almond mixture and beat together. Fold the flour and cocoa powder into the chocolate until smooth and, finally, fold in the meringue. Spread the mixture onto the baking tray (sheet) and bake in the oven for about 15 minutes or until the sponge springs back when pressed. Remove from the tray (sheet) and leave to cool on a wire rack.

Second, make the Alhambra sponge:

3 Preheat the oven to 180°C (350°F/ Gas 4). Line two 25.5 × 30cm (10 × 12 inch) baking trays (sheets) with non-stick baking mats. Melt the butter

continues

Orange & Chocolate Sacher
continued

in a pan and put the flour, cornflour (cornstarch) and cocoa powder into a bowl. Heat the eggs, egg yolks and sugar over a bain-marie (water bath) to 40°C (104°F), mixing continuously until ribbon stage (see page 218). Transfer this sabayon to a large bowl.

4 Add a small amount of the sabayon to the melted butter and mix until smooth, then fold two-thirds of the flour, cornflour (cornstarch) and cocoa powder into the remaining sabayon. Gently mix in the butter mixture and continue to fold in the dry ingredients until a smooth mixture is formed. Spread onto the prepared baking trays (sheets) with a palette knife and bake in the oven for 12–15 minutes until the sponge springs back when pressed. Remove from the baking trays (sheets) and leave to cool on a wire rack.

Next, make the orange jam:

5 Put the rind and chopped flesh into a saucepan with the orange juice and jam sugar. Bring to the boil and simmer for 5 minutes. Transfer to a food processor and blend for 5 minutes until smooth, then return to the pan and bring back to the boil. Cook for 3–4 minutes on a low heat. Set aside to cool slightly.

For the Grand Marnier syrup:

6 Put the sugar and water in a pan. Scrape the seeds from the split vanilla pod (bean) into the water and drop in the empty pod too. Bring to the boil, allow to cool and then add the Grand Marnier. Strain.

For the orange ganache:

7 Put the chocolate into a large bowl. Put the orange juice in a pan and bring to the boil. Boil, uncovered, until it has reduced to 90ml (3fl oz/⅓ cup). Add the sugar and bring back to the boil, then gradually pour it over the chopped chocolate, stirring to form an emulsion Add the butter and mix until smooth.

Finally, the orange & chocolate glaze:

8 Put the gelatine in enough cold water to just cover it, soak for a few minutes until soft and then squeeze off any excess water. Put the orange juice in a pan with the vanilla pod and seeds and bring to the boil. Boil, uncovered, until it has reduced to 250ml (9fl oz/1 cup). Add the sugar and bring back to the boil, then take it off the heat, add the gelatine and stir until dissolved. Pass through a fine sieve (strainer) into a bowl containing the chocolate and mix until smooth. Use straight away or store in an airtight container in the fridge until needed.

To assemble & finish:

9 Cut 2 rectangles of sacher sponge and 4 rectangles of Alhambra sponge to fit the frames (see Notes, page 175) – you may need to patch pieces of the sponge together to make this size.

10 For each frame, place a sacher sponge in the base and soak with the Grand Marnier syrup. Spread the orange ganache evenly on top, then chill for 10 minutes. Place one-quarter of the Chocolate Mousse on top of the ganache and then a rectangle of Alhambra sponge. Soak with syrup and chill for 10 minutes. Spread with half the jam and then top with the final Alhambra sponges, soak in syrup and chill for 10 minutes. Top with the remaining chocolate mousse, level off with a palette knife and transfer to the freezer to set, ideally overnight.

11 Demould the sachers. Gently warm the glaze (if necessary) and spoon generously over the top. Leave to set for about 1 hour, then cut into 4cm (1½ inch) slices. Trim the ends. Place on a serving dish and decorate with chocolate decorations and edible gold leaf.

BLACK FOREST

This is a German cake, so named because the kirsch originally used in the cake was produced in the Black Forest region. It is a very retro dessert – they were popular in the 1970s – and I love trying to recreate worn-out classics and give them another flush of life, making them as exciting as their first time around. This was a frequent feature on the menus at The River restaurant at The Savoy where I worked for Anton Edelmann. It is all about good-quality ingredients – if you use the best you're guaranteed a good cake.

Makes 4 x 4–6-portion servings

1 quantity **Fine Dark (Bittersweet) Chocolate Mousse – Anglaise Method** *(see page 160)*
½ quantity **Alhambra Sponge** *(see page 175)*
1 quantity **Kirsch Syrup** *(see page 193)*

For the biscuit moelleux sponge
45g (1½oz) fine dark (bittersweet) chocolate (65% cocoa solids), finely chopped
50g (1¾oz/⅓ cup) icing (powdered/pure) sugar, sifted
20g (¾oz/1 tbsp) cocoa powder, sifted
110g (4oz/1⅓ cups) ground almonds
10g (¼oz) cornflour (cornstarch)
85g (3oz/generous ⅓ cup) caster (superfine) sugar
90ml (3fl oz/⅓ cup) milk
55g (scant 2oz) egg yolks (almost 3 eggs)
160g (5½oz) egg whites (about 8 eggs)

For the white chocolate & kirsch mousse
8g (¼oz) leaf gelatine
140ml (4½fl oz/generous ½ cup) milk
½ vanilla pod (bean), split lengthways
175g (6oz) fine white chocolate, finely chopped
50ml (1¾fl oz/3 tbsp) kirsch
200ml (7fl oz/generous ¾ cup) whipping (pouring) cream (30% butter fat)

For the cherry compote
12g (2 tsp) pectin powder
35g (generous 1oz) caster (superfine) sugar
¼ cinnamon stick
200g (7oz) whole cherries (fresh or frozen), stoned and roughly chopped
100g (3½oz) ready-made cherry purée (or see Blackcurrant Purée, page 124)

To finish
1 quantity **Chocolate Cocoa Butter Solution** *(see page 29)*
Chocolate decorations *(see pages 152–157)*
Griottine cherries *(see page 224)*
Edible gold leaf

Notes:
- You will need four 14.5 × 4cm (5¾ × 1½ inch) bubble-top moulds *(see page 224)* and a spray gun *(see page 224)*.
- Both sponges can be made in advance and frozen.
- All other components should be made the same day.

First, make the moelleux sponge:

1 Preheat the oven to 180°C (350°F/Gas 4) and line a baking tray (sheet) with a non-stick baking mat. Melt the chocolate over a bain-marie (water bath) to 45°C (113°F). Put the sifted icing (powdered/pure) sugar and cocoa powder in a bowl and mix in the ground almonds.

2 In a saucepan mix together the cornflour (cornstarch) and 30g (1oz) of the caster (superfine) sugar, add the milk and mix to a paste. Cook over a low heat for 2 minutes, stirring continuously until thickened. Take the pan off the heat and mix in the egg yolks. Add half of the melted chocolate and mix well. Gradually add the remaining chocolate and mix until smooth.

3 In a mixing bowl, slowly whisk the egg whites, gradually adding the remaining sugar and increasing the speed. Continue to whisk to a soft peak meringue. Alternatively, whisk the egg whites in an electric mixer fitted with the whisk attachment. Fold the meringue into the chocolate mixture and then fold in the dry ingredients. Spoon the mixture into a piping (pastry) bag fitted with a 12mm (½ inch) plain nozzle (tip) and pipe four 15cm (6 inch) discs onto the prepared tray (sheet). Bake in the oven for about 15 minutes until it becomes slightly firmer around the edges, then leave to cool on a wire rack.

Next, make the white chocolate & kirsch mousse:

4 Soak the gelatine in enough cold water to just cover for a few minutes until soft, then gently squeeze off any excess water. Put the milk in a saucepan. Scrape the seeds from the

continues

Black Forest
continued

split vanilla pod (bean) into the milk, drop in the empty pod and bring to the boil. Take off the heat, add the gelatine and stir until dissolved. Pass through a sieve (strainer) into a bowl containing the chopped white chocolate and stir until melted and fully combined. Add the kirsch, then leave to thicken, stirring occasionally.

5 Lightly whip the cream until it forms soft peaks and then fold this into the white chocolate and kirsch mixture. Spoon into an airtight container and chill for at least 1 hour in the fridge or until needed.

Meanwhile, make the cherry compote:

6 Mix the pectin and the sugar together in a bowl. Put the cinnamon stick, chopped cherries and cherry purée in a saucepan and bring to the boil. Stir in the sugar and pectin and cook for 2–3 minutes over a low heat. Leave to cool.

To assemble & finish:

7 Cut the Alhambra sponge into 4 discs 12cm (5 inches) in diameter. Spoon the Fine Dark (Bittersweet) Chocolate Mousse into the 4 upside-down bubble-top moulds *(see Note, page 177)*, filling one-quarter full (about 250g/9oz in each). Use a palette knife to evenly spread the mousse and fill in all the gaps and up the sides of the moulds. Transfer to the freezer to set for 10 minutes.

8 Spoon the white chocolate and kirsch mousse into a piping (pastry) bag, snip a hole in the end and pipe a layer of the white chocolate mousse on top of the chocolate mousse (about 100g/3½oz in each). Transfer to the freezer again, for another 10 minutes.

9 Spoon a generous layer of the cherry compote on top of the mousse. Place an Alhambra sponge disc on top of the compote in each mould and liberally soak with the kirsch syrup. Spread a thin layer of the chocolate mousse on top of the sponge. Finally, place a biscuit moelleux sponge on top of each mould and brush liberally with more kirsch syrup. Transfer the moulds to the freezer and leave to set overnight.

10 To demould, dip the moulds into a bowl of hot water for no longer than 30 seconds. Turn them upside down onto a baking tray (sheet) lined with silicone (baking) paper, remove the mould and return the tray (sheet) to the freezer for 20 minutes.

11 To spray, place the baking tray (sheet) in a clear area. Fill a spray gun *(see page 224)* with the chocolate cocoa butter solution and, from a distance of around 1 metre (40 inches), spray the entremets with a continuous motion, turning to ensure a good coverage.

12 Place the entremets onto a serving dish and transfer to the fridge for 2–3 hours before serving. Decorate with chocolate squares and curls, Griottine cherries and gold leaf.

Makes 4 x 4-portion servings

½ quantity **Crystallized Almonds**
  (follow the Suisse Rochers recipe on page 102 up to the end of step 4)
½ quantity **Nutty Dacquoise**
  (see pages 36–37)
1 quantity **Genoise Sponge**
  (see page 126)
½ quantity **Blackcurrant Compote**
  (see Cherry Compote, page 177: make with 100g (3½oz) blackcurrants, 200g (7oz) blackcurrant purée, 5g (1tsp) pectin and 35g (1oz) caster (superfine) sugar)
1 quantity **Blackcurrant Mousse**
  (see Apricot Mousse, page 170: make with 125g (4½oz) blackcurrant purée, 150ml (5fl oz/⅔ cup) cream, 4g (¾ tsp) leaf gelatine and 25g (scant 1oz) sugar)
2 quantities **Chocolate Glasage** *(see page 165), made using 400g (14oz) milk chocolate and omitting the sugar*
Chocolate decorations *(see pages 152–157) and edible gold leaf, to finish*

For the red wine poached pears

350ml (12fl oz/scant 1½ cups) red wine
60g (2oz/¼ cup) caster (superfine) sugar
½ vanilla pod (bean), split lengthways
3 pears (Roka), peeled, cored and
  quartered

For the milk chocolate mousse

2g (¼ tsp) leaf gelatine
75ml (2½fl oz/scant ⅓ cup) milk
345ml (12fl oz/1⅓ cups) whipping
  (pouring) cream (30% butter fat)
30g (1oz) egg yolks (about 1½ eggs)
20g (¾oz) caster (superfine) sugar
310g (10½oz) fine milk chocolate,
  finely chopped

BLACKCURRANT, PEAR & MILK CHOCOLATE ENTREMET

This entremet was created after a visit to some of Paris's finest chocolateries.

First, make the poached pears:

1 Put the red wine, water and sugar in a saucepan. Scrape the vanilla seeds from the pod (bean) and add the pod, bring to the boil, then reduce the heat to simmer. Add the pears to the simmering syrup and place a disc of silicone (baking) paper on top. Poach at a gentle simmer for about 30 minutes or until soft. Take off the heat, cool and place in an airtight container. Store in the fridge overnight.

Second, make the chocolate mousse:

2 Soak the gelatine in enough cold water to cover it for a few minutes until soft and then gently squeeze off any excess water. Set aside. Place the milk and 50ml (1¾fl oz/3 tbsp) of the cream in a pan and bring to the boil.

3 In a separate bowl, whisk the egg yolks and sugar together until light in colour, about 2–3 minutes. Pour half the boiled milk over the egg yolk mixture, combine thoroughly, then return to the milk in the pan. Cook over a low heat, stirring continuously until the mixture is thick enough to coat the back of a spoon. Take off the heat, add the gelatine and stir until fully combined. Pass through a sieve (strainer) into a bowl containing the chopped chocolate, stir until fully combined and leave to cool. Lightly whip the rest of the cream and fold into the chocolate mixture. Use immediately.

> **Notes:**
> • You will need four 14.5 × 7cm (5¾ × 2¾ inch) oval frames *(see page 224).*
> • The dacquoise and sponge can be made in advance and frozen.

To assemble & finish:

4 Cut 4 ovals of the nutty dacquoise to fit your frames *(see Note, below)* and place one in the base of each frame. Cut 4 ovals of the Genoise sponge about 1cm (½ inch) smaller and set aside. For each frame, spread one-quarter of the blackcurrant compote onto the dacquoise base. Spoon about 100g (3½oz) of the milk chocolate mousse into each frame and use a small angled palette knife to thinly cover the base and up the sides of the frame. Transfer to the freezer for about 20 minutes to set. Remove the pears from the syrup and leave to dry on a cloth to remove any excess liquid. Cut the pears into 1.5cm (¾ inch) cubes.

5 Place the cut sponge in the frames, brush with the poaching syrup and evenly distribute the pears on top. Spoon the blackcurrant mousse into a piping (pastry) bag, snip a small hole in the end and fill up to 2cm (¾ inch) from the top of the frames. Top each with one-quarter of the remaining chocolate mousse, using a palette knife to ensure you have no air pockets and to level off the top. Return to the freezer and leave to set, ideally overnight.

6 Demould the entremets and return them to the freezer. Gently heat the chocolate glaze to 40°C (104°F), then cool to about 28–30°C (83–86°F). Take the entremets from the freezer and place onto a wire rack with a tray below. Pour the glaze over the entremets, ensuring all the sides are covered. Chill for about 1 hour until set. Remove from the glazing rack using a palette knife and put onto a serving dish. Place the almonds around the entremets base. Finish with chocolate decorations and gold leaf.

RASPBERRY DELICE

The sharpness of the raspberry cuts beautifully through the richness of the chocolate in this traditional French patisserie.

Makes about 16 slices

1 quantity Kirsch Syrup *(see page 193)*
1 quantity Raspberry Ganache
   (see Orange Ganache, page 175),
   made with 200g (7oz) raspberry purée
   instead of the reduced orange juice and
   35g (1oz) caster (superfine) sugar
1 quantity Raspberry Compote
   (see Cherry Compote, page 177),
   made with 100g (3½oz) each of
   raspberries and raspberry purée
   and 30g (1oz) jam sugar
1 quantity Chocolate Mousse –
   Anglaise Method *(see page 160)*

For the rich chocolate sponge

115g (4oz) fine dark (bittersweet)
   chocolate (66% cocoa solids),
   finely chopped
60g (2oz/5 tbsp) unsalted butter, cubed
50g (1¾oz) egg yolks (about 2½ eggs)
115g (4oz) egg whites (about 4 eggs)
60g (2oz/¼ cup) caster (superfine) sugar
20g (¾oz) plain (all-purpose) flour, sifted

For the flourless chocolate sponge

200g (7oz) egg whites (about 6½ eggs)
180g (6½oz/¾ cup) caster
   (superfine) sugar
130g (4½oz) egg yolks (about 6 eggs)
60g (2oz/scant ⅔ cup) cocoa powder,
   sifted

For the seedy raspberry glaze

5g (¾ tsp) leaf gelatine
30g (1oz) caster (superfine) sugar
50ml (1¾fl oz/3 tbsp) water
100g (3½oz) raspberry purée
   (see Blackcurrant Purée, page 124)
75g (2½oz) raspberries

To finish

Chocolate decorations
   (see pages 152–153)
Edible gold leaf
Fresh raspberries

First, make the rich chocolate sponge:

1 Preheat the oven to 180°C (350°F/ Gas 4) and line a 25.5 × 30cm (10 × 12 inch) baking tray (sheet) with a non-stick baking mat. Melt the chopped chocolate over a bain-marie (water bath). Add in the cubed butter and mix until fully melted and incorporated. Stir in the egg yolks and mix until smooth.

2 In a mixing bowl, whisk the egg whites, gradually adding the sugar and increasing the speed. Continue to whisk to a soft peak meringue. Alternatively, whisk in an electric mixer fitted with a whisk attachment. Fold the meringue into the chocolate mixture, then fold in the flour. Spread out evenly onto the prepared tray (sheet). Bake in the oven for 15–18 minutes until the cake springs back when lightly pressed. Leave to cool on a wire rack.

Second, make the flourless sponge:

3 Preheat the oven to 200°C (400°F/ Gas 6) and line two 25.5 × 30cm (10 × 12 inch) baking trays (sheets) with non-stick baking mats. In a mixing bowl, whisk the egg whites, gradually adding the sugar and increasing the speed. Continue to whisk to a soft peak meringue. Alternatively, whisk in an electric mixer fitted with a whisk attachment. Gradually add the egg yolks and mix until fully incorporated. Fold in the cocoa powder. Spread into the prepared baking trays (sheets) and bake in the oven for 10–12 minutes. Leave to cool on a wire rack.

Next, make the raspberry glaze:

4 Soak the gelatine in enough cold water to just cover it for a few minutes until soft and then squeeze

out any excess water. Put the sugar, water, raspberry purée and whole raspberries in a saucepan and bring to the boil. Mix to break down the raspberries. Take off the heat, add the gelatine and stir to dissolve. Leave to cool, then store in an airtight container until needed.

To assemble and finish:

5 You will need two 37 × 9 × 4cm (15 × 3½ × 1½ inch) mousse frames *(see page 224)*. Cut 2 rectangles of rich chocolate sponge and 4 rectangles of flourless chocolate sponge to fit the frames – you may need to patch pieces of the sponge together to make this size.

6 For each frame, place a chocolate sponge into the base of the frame, soak well with kirsch syrup and spread half the raspberry ganache evenly on top. Chill for 10 minutes. Place a rectangle of flourless sponge on top of the ganache and soak generously with more kirsch syrup. Spread a thin layer of the raspberry compote on top of this. Spoon one-quarter of the Chocolate Mousse on top and use an angled palette knife to spread out evenly. Place a final sheet of flourless chocolate sponge on top, soak generously with the kirsch syrup and spread a thin layer of compote on top. Top up with the rest of the chocolate mousse, level off with a palette knife and transfer to the freezer to set, ideally overnight.

7 To finish, demould the entremets. Gently warm the glaze (if necessary) and spoon generously over the top. Chill for about 1 hour to set and cut into 4cm (1½ inch) slices. Trim the ends. Place on a serving dish and decorate with chocolate decorations, edible gold leaf and fresh raspberries.

MATCHA & DARK CHOCOLATE ENTREMET

This combination came from one of our many trips to visit the patisseries of Japan. We're inspired by the new wave of innovative Japanese patissiers whose attention to detail in reproducing French classical patisserie is astonishing. They are leading a revolution as patisserie becomes an increasingly important part of the Japanese culture. The citrus flavours from the yuzu and orange work beautifully with the matcha crème brûlée and chocolate mousse.

Makes 15

1 quantity Flourless Chocolate Sponge
(see page 182)
1 quantity Grand Marnier Syrup
(see page 175)
1 quantity Chocolate Mousse – Sabayon
Method (see page 161)
1 quantity Orange Marmalade (see page
126), but replace 100g (3½oz) of the
oranges with fresh yuzu (or a mix of
half lime and mandarin)
Chocolate decorations (see pages
152–157) and edible gold leaf, to finish

For the matcha crème brûlée
250g (9fl oz/1 cup) whipping
(pouring) cream
½ vanilla pod (bean), split lengthways
50g (1¾oz) egg yolks (about 2½ eggs)
40g (1½oz) caster (superfine) sugar
6g (1 tsp) matcha (green tea powder)

For the praline feuillantine
150g (5½oz) fine milk chocolate
(32% cocoa solids), finely chopped
115g (4oz) Praline Paste
(see pages 158–159)
140g (5oz) feuillantine wafers
(see page 224)

For the chocolate glasage
18g (¾oz) leaf gelatine
235ml (8fl oz/scant 1 cup) water
300g (10oz/1⅓ cups) caster
(superfine) sugar
100g (3½oz/1 cup) cocoa powder, sifted
170ml (6fl oz/generous ⅔ cup) whipping
(pouring) cream

First, make the matcha crème brûlée:

1 Preheat the oven to 130°C (250°F/
Gas ½) and place a silicone baking mat
with 1.5cm (¾ inch) cavities (see page
224) into a shallow baking tray (sheet).
Put the cream in a saucepan, scrape
the vanilla seeds into the pan and add
in the vanilla pod (bean). Bring to the
boil. Meanwhile, put the egg yolks in a
mixing bowl, add the sugar and matcha
powder and whisk until it becomes
lighter in colour.

2 Pour half of the hot cream onto
the egg yolk mixture and mix together.
Add the rest of the cream, then pass
through a fine sieve (strainer). Pour the
mixture into the cavities, fill the tray
(sheet) close to the top of the mould
with water and bake in the oven for
15–20 minutes or until the custard
just sets and if you shake them gently
they wobble like jelly in the middle.
Leave to cool, then carefully remove
the mat from the tray (sheet), place
onto another baking tray and freeze for
about 2–3 hours or until frozen.

Notes:
- You will need 15 metal triangle
  moulds that are 4.5cm (1¾ inch)
  deep with 6.5cm (2¾ inch) sides
  (see page 224).
- The sponge, marmalade and
  brulée can be made in advance.
  The sponge can be frozen and
  the marmalade should be kept in
  the fridge.
- All other components should be
  made the same day.

Second, make the praline feuillantine:

3 Melt the chocolate over a bain-
marie (water bath) to 45°C (113°F).
Mix in the praline paste and feuillantine
wafer. Spread 3mm (⅛ inch) thick
onto a baking tray (sheet) lined with
silicone (baking) paper. Leave to set,
break into small pieces or shards and
store in an airtight container until
needed.

Next, make the chocolate glasage:

4 Soak the gelatine in enough cold
water to just cover for a few minutes
until soft, then gently squeeze off
any excess water. Put the water and
sugar in a saucepan, bring to the boil
and continue to cook over a low
heat for 2–3 minutes. Add the sifted
cocoa powder and the cream. Bring
back to the boil and then simmer for
4–5 minutes. Take the pan off the
heat, add the gelatine and stir until
dissolved. Pass through a fine sieve
(strainer) and leave to cool.

To assemble & finish:

5 De-mould the frozen crème brûlée
and place them back in the freezer.
Cut 15 triangles of the flourless
chocolate sponge to fit in the base
of the triangular entremet moulds
(see Note, opposite). Use a 3.5cm
(1½ inch) round cutter to cut 15
flourless chocolate sponge discs for
the centre of the entremets.

continues

Matcha & Dark Chocolate Entremet
continued

6 Place a base triangle sponge in each mould and soak with Grand Marnier syrup. Place enough Chocolate Mousse in the moulds to line the sides and base using a small palette knife.

7 Place 3 small pieces of praline feuillantine in the centre of eachmousse. Then place the round sponge discs on top and soak with Grand Marnier syrup. Place a generous spoonful of the yuzu & orange marmalade onto each disc of chocolate sponge and put the matcha crème brûlée on top of this. Top up the moulds with the chocolate mousse and level off with a palette knife. Transfer to the freezer for about 2–3 hours or until frozen.

8 Demould the entremets and return to the freezer. Melt the chocolate glasage gently to about 40–45°C (104–113°F), then leave to cool to 23–25°C (73–75°F). Take the entremets from the freezer and place them onto a wire rack with a tray below (see pic opposite). Pour the chocolate glasage over the entremets, ensuring all the sides are covered with the glasage. Leave to set for about 1 hour in the fridge. Using a small angled palette knife remove the entremets from the wire rack and place on a serving dish. Finish with chocolate decorations and edible gold leaf.

CHOCOLATE & PRALINE PARIS BREST

This wonderful patisserie was first created to commemorate the bicycle race between Paris and Brest, which dates back to 1891. Confusion remains as to the exact creator, but he was clearly a very crafty baker. On seeing the first race, he was so inspired that he created this tyre-shaped choux pastry filled with praline crème patisserie and crème Chantilly, mimicking the newly invented inner tubes of the day and topped with roasted almonds and icing (powdered/pure) sugar to represent the dust from the road. This Pastry of Champions soon became a favourite amongst the riders and is now a regular fixture in many patisserie shops across France.

Makes 15–16

For the choux pastry
125ml (4fl oz/½ cup) water
125ml (4fl oz/½ cup) milk
125g (4½oz) unsalted butter,
   cut into cubes
12g (⅓oz) caster (superfine) sugar
160g (5½oz/1 cup) plain (all-purpose)
   flour, sifted
2g (¼ tsp) salt
250g (9oz) whole eggs (about 5 eggs),
   beaten
Egg wash *(see page 144)*
100g (3½oz/1 cup) flaked almonds

For the praline crémeux
225ml (7½fl oz/scant 1 cup)
   whipping (pouring) cream
100ml (3½fl oz/generous ⅓ cup) milk
80g (2¾oz) egg yolks (about 4 eggs)
30g (1oz) caster (superfine) sugar
180g (6½oz) fine dark (bittersweet)
   chocolate (65% cocoa solids),
   finely chopped
75g (2½ oz) gianduja *(see page 224)*,
   finely chopped
75g (2½oz) **Praline Paste**
   (see pages 158–159)
25g (scant 1oz) unsalted butter,
   softened

For the chocolate pastry cream
500ml (16fl oz/2 cups) milk
½ vanilla pod (bean), split lengthways
120g (4¼oz) egg yolks (about 6 eggs)
100g (3½oz/generous ½ cup)
   caster (superfine) sugar
40g (1½oz/scant ⅓ cup) plain
   (all-purpose) flour, sifted
40g (1½oz/¼ cup) cocoa powder
50g (1¾oz) fine dark (bittersweet)
   chocolate (70% cocoa solids)

To finish
80g (2¾oz/¾ cup) hazelnuts,
   roughly chopped
2 quantities **Crème Chantilly**
   (see page 162)
Icing (powdered/pure) sugar, to dust
Chocolate decorations
   (see pages 152–157)

Notes:
• You may end up with more choux pastry than you need – it can be baked as choux rings and then stored in an airtight container in the freezer (but you must crisp them up in the oven before use).

First, make the choux pastry:

1 Preheat the oven to 200°C (400°F/Gas 6). Heat the water, milk, butter and sugar in a saucepan. Bring up to the boil for about 1 minute. Take the pan off the heat, and add the sifted flour and salt. Use a spatula to stir until completely combined. Return the pan to the hob, reduce the heat to low and continue stirring with a spatula until the choux dough leaves the sides of the pan. Take off the heat and leave the dough to cool, for 2–3 minutes, stirring occasionally.

2 Gradually add the beaten eggs into the dough and mix until smooth. Transfer the choux dough to a piping (pastry) bag fitted with a 14mm (¾ inch) plain nozzle (tip). Pipe 15–16 rings measuring 6cm (2½ inches) in diameter onto a baking tray (sheet) lined with a non-stick baking mat (you may have to bake in batches). Carefully brush the rings with the egg wash. Sprinkle over the flaked almonds and dust away any excess.

3 Bake the choux rings for 20 minutes. Reduce the temperature to 160°C (325°F/Gas 3) and bake for a further 10–15 minutes until golden. Do not open the oven during baking as the rings may collapse. Remove from the oven and leave to cool on a wire rack.

continues

Chocolate & Praline Paris Brest
continued

Second, make the praline crémeux:

4 In a saucepan, heat the cream and milk until boiling. In a mixing bowl, whisk together the egg yolks and sugar until light in colour, about 2–3 minutes. Pour half of the boiling liquid into the egg mixture, whisk until mixed through and then transfer all of the egg yolk mixture back to the saucepan. Continuously stir until the custard is thick enough to coat the back of a spoon, taking care not to overcook. Take off the heat, pass through a fine sieve (strainer) into a bowl containing the chopped chocolates and praline paste and stir until fully incorporated. Add the butter and mix until smooth. Pour into a shallow dish, wrap with cling film (plastic wrap), cool rapidly and leave to fully set.

Third, make the chocolate pastry cream:

5 Put the milk and the half vanilla pod (bean) in a saucepan and bring to the boil. In a mixing bowl, whisk together the egg yolks and sugar. Continue whisking until the mixture slightly thickens and turns light in colour, 2–3 minutes. Add the sifted flour and cocoa powder and whisk again until smooth.

6 Pour half of the infused milk into the mixing bowl and whisk again until there are no lumps. Pass this mixture through a fine sieve (strainer), then return the mixture back to the remaining milk in the pan. Continuously whisk the mixture until it comes to a boil, then reduce the temperature to a simmer. Continue to stir and cook for 5–6 minutes.

7 Take off the heat, add in the chocolate and stir until it has completely melted. Pour the pastry cream onto a shallow dish or tray, wrap with cling film (plastic wrap) and cool rapidly.

To assemble & finish:

8 Preheat the oven to 180°C (350°F/ Gas 4). Carefully slice the choux rings in half horizontally (if you are using frozen choux rings, you will need to defrost them and pop them in the oven to crisp up for 2–3 minutes) and set on baking trays (sheets). Place the baking trays (sheets) in the oven for 1–2 minutes to crisp up. (Skip the baking if you are using the choux rings the same day they were made). Remove and leave to cool.

9 Spoon the praline crémeux into a piping (pastry) bag fitted with a 12mm (½ inch) plain nozzle (tip) and pipe a ring on top of each choux ring base. Sprinkle with the chopped hazelnuts.

10 Spoon the chocolate pastry cream into a piping (pastry) bag fitted with a 12mm (½ inch) plain nozzle (tip) and use it to pipe a layer of cream on top of the praline crémeux. Spoon the crème Chantilly into another piping (pastry) bag fitted with a 10mm (½ inch) fluted nozzle (tip) and pipe swirls on top of the pastry cream.

11 Top with the other halves of the choux rings and press down slightly so that the lids are stable. Pipe a rosette of crème Chantilly on top of each ring, dust lightly with icing (powdered/ pure) sugar and decorate with chocolate decorations.

Notes:
- Leftover pastry can be kept in the fridge for a few days or frozen.
- You will need 12 tartlet tins 7cm (2¾ inches) in diameter and 3cm (1½ inches) deep *(see page 224)*.

SEA SALT CARAMEL TARTS

Sea salt caramel has become incredibly popular and this dish, along with products like the sea salt caramel spread and ice cream, were created to meet this interest. The sharpness of the raspberries offsets the richness of the sea salt caramel, and the chocolate on top brings it all together. The hazelnut pastry brings a crispy contrast.

Makes 12 tarts

½ quantity Sea Salt Caramel
   (see page 79)
75g (2½oz/½ cup) hazelnuts, chopped
1 quantity Raspberry Compote
   (see page 182)
Twelve 6cm (2½ inch) chocolate discs
   (see Flat Sheet Techniques, page 157)
Chocolate decorations *(see pages
   152–157)*, edible gold leaf, chopped
   hazelnuts and halved raspberries,
   to finish

For the hazelnut & almond pastry
225g (8oz/2¼ sticks) unsalted butter,
   cut into cubes
135g (5oz/generous¾ cup) icing
   (powdered/pure) sugar, sifted
50g (1¾oz/⅔ cup) ground hazelnuts
50g (1¾oz/⅔ cup) ground almonds
2g (¼ tsp) salt
75g (2½oz) eggs (about 1½ eggs), beaten
325g (11oz/2¼ cups) soft flour, sifted

For the raspberry dacquoise
125g (4½oz/1⅔ cups) ground almonds
60g (2oz) icing (powdered/pure) sugar
30g (1oz) plain (all-purpose) flour
160g (5½oz) egg whites (about 5 eggs)
125g (4½oz/generous ½ cup) caster
   (superfine) sugar
125g (4½oz) frozen raspberries, chopped

For the dark chocolate crémeux
150ml (5fl oz/⅔ cup) whipping
   (pouring) cream
75ml (2½fl oz/scant ⅓ cup) milk
55g (scant 2oz) egg yolks (about 3 eggs)
25g (scant 1oz) caster (superfine) sugar
160g (5½oz) fine dark (bittersweet)
   chocolate (66% cocoa solids),
   roughly chopped
15g (½oz) unsalted butter, softened

First, make the pastry:

1 Put the butter in a mixing bowl and add the icing sugar. Beat together until light in colour. Mix in the ground nuts and the salt. Beat until smooth. Gradually add the eggs. Lastly, add the flour and mix to form a smooth and homogenous mass. Place the pastry onto a floured baking tray (sheet), wrap in cling film (plastic wrap) and chill for at least 1 hour. Roll out the pastry on a lightly floured surface to 3mm (⅛ inch) thick and line 12 tartlet cases. Prick the base of the tarts and leave to rest for at least 1 hour.

Meanwhile, make the dacquoise:

2 Preheat the oven to 160°C (325°F/ Gas 3). Mix together the almonds, icing sugar and flour. Meanwhile, in the bowl of an electric mixer, whisk the egg whites, gradually adding the sugar and increasing the speed. Continue to whisk to a firm meringue *(see page 218)*. Alternatively, whisk by hand. Fold the dry ingredients and the raspberries into the meringue. Spread the mixture onto a 25.5 × 30cm (10 × 12 inch) baking tray lined with silicone (baking) paper. Bake in the oven for 18–20 minutes. Leave to cool, then cut into 5cm (2 inch) discs with a plain cutter.

Next, make the chocolate crémeux:

3 Put the cream and milk in a saucepan and bring to the boil. Meanwhile, whisk the egg yolks and sugar together in a mixing bowl until light in colour, about 2–3 minutes. Pour half of the boiled cream over the egg yolks, mix and then return to the

cream in the pan. Cook over a low heat until the custard is thick enough to coat the back of a spoon, being careful not to overcook. Take off the heat and pass through a fine sieve (strainer) into a bowl containing the chopped chocolate and mix gently until the chocolate has melted. Add the butter and mix until smooth. Pour into a shallow dish, cover with cling film (plastic wrap) and cool rapidly until firm.

Next, bake the pastry:

4 Preheat the oven to 180°C (350°F/ Gas 4). Line the tartlets with silicone (baking) paper and fill with baking beans. Bake for 12–15 minutes, remove the beans and bake for 8–10 minutes more. Leave for 5 minutes, then remove from the cases and cool on a rack.

To assemble & finish:

5 Spoon the sea salt caramel into a piping (pastry) bag, snip a small hole in the end and pipe a small bulb into the base of each tartlet case. Sprinkle about 1 teaspoon of chopped hazelnuts on top of the caramel. Spoon a layer of the raspberry compote on top, then a disc of raspberry dacquoise. Pipe a ring of caramel around the edge of the disc and then spoon on a small amount of compote. Top with a chocolate disc.

6 Stir the crémeux to loosen and spoon into a piping (pastry) bag fitted with a 7mm (¼ inch) plain nozzle (tip). Pipe spirals of cremeux on top of the chocolate. Decorate with raspberries, chocolate decoration, hazelnuts and gold leaf.

PISTACHIO & CHOCOLATE OPERA

The first Opera was created in the 1930s by Louis Clichy for a reception held at the Paris Opera House. Traditionally it is made with layers of sponge and buttercream and flavoured with chocolate and coffee. Here we use Sicilian pistachios, cherries and chocolate and a crème mousseline. As a business we believe that training apprentices and young chefs is very important and this is a great dish for newcomers to learn as it covers many basic skills – assembling the Opera to a high standard is a skill on its own. I was first taught how to make the perfect Opera by Willie Pike, a fellow Scottish chef.

Makes 14–16 slices

2 quantities Chocolate Glasage
  (see page 165)
Chocolate decorations (see pages
  152–157) and edible gold leaf,
  to finish

For the pistachio macaroons
(Makes about 50 small macaroons)
120g (4½oz) egg whites (about 4 eggs)
125g (4½oz/generous ½ cup) caster
  (superfine) sugar
125g (4½oz/1⅔ cups) ground almonds
125g (4½oz/¾ cup) icing
  (powdered) sugar
35g (generous 1¼oz) Pistachio Paste
  (see page 52)
Chopped pistachios, to decorate

For the pistachio joconde sponge
50g (1¾oz/⅔ cup) ground almonds
300g (10oz/1⅓ cups) caster
  (superfine) sugar
200g (7oz) egg whites (about 7 eggs)
85g (3oz) Pistachio Paste (see page 52)
75g (2½oz/½ cup) icing (powdered/
  pure) sugar
60g (2oz) egg yolks (about 3 eggs)
100g (3½oz) cornflour (cornstarch)
45g (1½oz/4 tbsp) unsalted butter,
  melted and cooled

For the kirsch syrup
180ml (6fl oz/¾ cup) water
170g (6oz/¾ cup) caster
  (superfine) sugar
½ vanilla pod (bean), split lengthways
150ml (5fl oz/⅔ cup) kirsch

For the pistachio crème mousseline
335ml (11fl oz/1⅓ cups) milk
1 vanilla pod (bean), split lengthways
80g (2¾oz) egg yolks (about 4 eggs)
65g (2oz/generous ¼ cup) caster
  (superfine) sugar
35g (generous 1¼oz) plain (all-purpose)
  flour, sifted
165g (5½oz/1⅔ sticks) unsalted butter,
  cut into cubes and at room temperature
40g (1½oz) Pistachio Paste (see page 52)

For the cherry ganache
400g (14oz) ready-made cherry purée
  (or see Blackcurrant Purée, page 124)
80g (2¾oz/generous ⅓ cup) caster
  (superfine) sugar
300g (10oz) milk chocolate, chopped
300g (10oz) fine dark (bittersweet)
  chocolate (65% cocoa solids), chopped
100g (3½oz/1 stick) unsalted butter,
  softened

Notes:
- You will need two 37 × 9 × 4cm (15 × 3½ × 1½ inch) mousse frames *(see page 224)*.
- Any leftover macaroons and sponge can be frozen in an airtight container. The macaroons make perfect petit fours.
- Make the ganache and the glaze just before you are ready to assemble the Opera.

First, make the pistachio macaroons:

1 Preheat the oven to 150°C (300°F/ Gas 2) and line 2–3 baking trays (sheets) with non-stick baking mats. Mix together 60g (2oz) of the egg whites and the caster (superfine) sugar in a mixing bowl until the sugar is fully dissolved. Place the bowl over a bain-marie (water bath) and continue to whisk until the meringue is quite hot, about 60°C (140°F). Transfer the meringue mixture to an electric mixer fitted with the whisk attachment and continue to whisk until a stiff meringue forms *(see page 218)* and the mixture returns to room temperature, about 10 minutes.

2 Sieve together the ground almonds and icing (powdered/pure) sugar into a mixing bowl, add the remaining egg whites and pistachio paste and beat to a paste. Using a spatula, fold the meringue into the paste and mix until smooth. Spoon the mixture into a piping (pastry) bag fitted with a 8mm (¼ inch) plain nozzle (tip), pipe 2.5cm (1 inch) diameter bulbs onto the prepared trays (sheets) and sprinkle with chopped pistachios. Leave to dry out for about 20–25 minutes.

3 Bake in the preheated oven for 10 minutes, then lower the temperature to 140°C (275°F/ Gas 1) for a further 6–8 minutes.

continues

Pistachio & Chocolate Opera
continued

Second, make the pistachio sponge:

4 Preheat the oven to 180°C (350°F/Gas 4) and line three 25.5 × 30cm (10 × 12 inch) baking trays (sheets) with non-stick baking mats. In a mixing bowl, beat together the ground almonds, 90g (3oz/generous ½ cup) of the caster (superfine) sugar, 85g (3oz) of the egg whites and the pistachio paste until it binds together. Gradually mix in the icing (powdered/pure) sugar until smooth. Then add in the egg yolks and beat until smooth and light, for about 4–5 minutes. Mix in the cornflour (cornstarch) and the melted butter.

5 In an electric mixer, slowly whisk the remaining egg whites. Gradually increase the speed while adding the remaining sugar. Continue to whisk to a soft peak meringue. Alternatively, whisk by hand in a clean mixing bowl. Carefully fold the meringue into the pistachio base. Once the meringue is fully incorporated, spread an equal amount into each tray (sheet) used an angled palette knife. Bake in the oven for 15 minutes until golden on top and the sponge springs back when pressed.

Third, make the kirsch syrup:

6 Put the water and sugar in a saucepan, bring to the boil and then leave to cool. Add the kirsch, transfer to an airtight container and store in the fridge until needed.

And the pistachio crème mousseline:

7 Put the milk and the vanilla pod (bean) in a saucepan and bring to the boil. Meanwhile, whisk together the egg yolks and sugar in a mixing bowl. Continue to whisk until the mixture slightly thickens and turns light in colour, about 2–3 minutes. Add in the flour and whisk until smooth. Add half of the hot milk to the egg mixture and whisk until there are no lumps. Pass the mixture through a fine sieve (strainer) and return the mixture back to the pan.

8 Using a whisk, stir the mixture. When it comes to the boil, bring the temperature down to a simmer. Continue to stir and simmer for 5–6 minutes. Take off the heat and remove the vanilla pod (bean). Place the mixture in an electric mixer and beat on a low speed until it reaches room temperature (you may need to scrape down the sides a couple of times). Increase the speed and add the pistachio paste, then gradually add the butter, cube by cube, until it is fully combined. Store in an airtight container until needed.

Meanwhile, make the cherry ganache:

9 Put the cherry purée and sugar in a saucepan and bring to the boil. Pour into a bowl containing the chopped chocolate and using a spatula, mix to form an emulsion. Add the softened butter and mix until smooth. Leave to cool. Set aside one-quarter of the ganache to use for filling the macaroons.

To assemble & finish:

10 Spoon the reserved cherry ganache into a piping (pastry) bag, snip a small hole in the end and pipe a small amount onto the flat side of 16 of the macaroons. Sandwich together with another 16 halves, flat-side down.

11 Cut 6 rectangles of the pistachio sponge to fit the frames (see *Note*, page 193) – you may need to patch pieces of the sponge together to make this size.

12 For each frame, place a sponge rectangle in the base of the frame, lightly soak with kirsch syrup and spread one-quarter of the remaining cherry ganache on top. Chill for 10 minutes. Spread a layer of the pistachio crème mousseline on top of this, top with another sponge rectangle and generously soak with one-third of the kirsch syrup. Repeat with another layer of cherry ganache, chill for 10 minutes and then another layer of pistachio crème mousseline. Place the final sponge rectangle on top and generously soak with the remaining kirsch syrup. Transfer to the freezer to set, ideally overnight.

13 To finish, demould the Operas. Gently warm the chocolate glaze (if necessary) and spoon over the top. Chill for about 1 hour to set and cut into 4cm (1½ inch) slices. Trim the ends. Place on a serving dish and decorate with chocolate decorations, edible gold leaf and the pistachio macaroons.

CHOCOLATE TIRAMISU CASKET

We prepare our tiramisu in a chocolate casket to create a statuesque and impressive dish. It is a version of one of the desserts that I made with Suzue when we represented Scotland at the Culinary Olympics in 2004. We are still very proud to have been awarded Gold for our creations for Scotland.

Makes 12

Cocoa powder, to dust
Chopped cocoa nibs and 12 **Chocolate Copeaux** *(see page 153)*, to finish

For the chocolate jelly
4g (¾ tsp) leaf gelatine
250ml (9fl oz/1 cup) milk
20g (¾oz) caster (superfine) sugar
140g (5oz) fine dark (bittersweet) chocolate (70% cocoa solids), finely chopped

For the biscuit a la cuillere
(makes about 25 biscuits)
90g (3oz) egg whites (about 3 eggs)
95g (3½oz/scant ½ cup) caster (superfine) sugar
60g (2oz) egg yolks (about 3 eggs), beaten
95g (3½oz/⅔ cup) plain (all-purpose) flour, sifted

For the gold cocoa butter
20g (¾oz) cocoa butter, finely chopped
2g (¼ tsp) edible gold powder *(see page 224)*

For the espresso syrup
150ml (5fl oz/⅔ cup) strong espresso coffee
25g (scant 1oz) caster (superfine) sugar
60ml (2fl oz/¼ cup) dark rum

For the mascarpone mousse
60g (2oz) egg yolks (about 3 eggs)
100g (3½oz/scant ½ cup) caster (superfine) sugar
½ vanilla pod (bean), split lengthways
250ml (9fl oz/1 cup) double (heavy) cream (36% butter fat)
400g (14oz) mascarpone

For the chocolate casket
12 acetate sheets measuring 10 × 12cm (4 × 5 inches)
500g (1lb 2oz) tempered fine dark (bittersweet) chocolate *(see pages 18–19)*
Gold cocoa butter *(see opposite)*

Notes:
- You will need 12 acetate sheets each measuring 10 × 12cm (4 × 5 inches) *(see page 224)*.
- The biscuit can be made in advance and stored in an airtight container and the jelly and syrup can be made the day before and stored in the fridge until needed.

First, make the chocolate jelly:

1 Line a small shallow baking tray (sheet) with cling film (plastic wrap). Soak the gelatine in enough cold water to just cover it for a few minutes until soft squeeze off the excess water. Put the milk and sugar in a saucepan and bring to the boil. Add the gelatine and stir to dissolve.

2 Pour one-third of the milk into a bowl containing the chopped chocolate, mix until smooth and then add the rest of the milk and stir through. Pass through a fine sieve (strainer) into the prepared tray (sheet), leave to cool, then transfer to the fridge to set for at least 2 hours. Once set, use a 3cm (1½ inch) cutter to cut out 24 discs.

Second, make the biscuit à la cuillère:

3 Preheat the oven to 200°C (400°F/Gas 6) and line a baking tray (sheet) with a non-stick baking mat. In a mixing bowl, whisk the egg whites, gradually adding the sugar and increasing the speed. Continue to whisk to a soft peak meringue. Alternatively, whisk in an electric mixer fitted with a whisk attachment. Gradually pour in the beaten egg yolks and mix until fully incorporated. Fold in the sifted flour.

4 Spread the mixture onto the prepared baking mat using an angled palette knife and bake in the oven for 15–18 minutes until golden brown. Leave to cool on a wire rack, then use a 3cm (1½ inch) cutter to cut out at least 24 discs (you can either wrap and freeze any leftover dough or use up all of the dough and enjoy the biscuits on their own).

Third, make the gold cocoa butter:

5 Put the cocoa butter in a small bowl and melt gently over a bain-marie (water bath). Mix in the edible gold powder and leave to cool until it thickens slightly.

continues

Chocolate Tiramisu Casket
continued

Now, make the chocolate casket:

6 Place an acetate sheet *(see Note, page 195)* onto a flat baking tray (sheet) and secure with tape along one of the 10cm (4 inch) edges. Polish the surface with cotton wool. Using a pastry brush, coat the sheet with a line of gold cocoa butter from the bottom left-hand corner diagonally up to the top right-hand corner. Repeat with the remaining acetate sheets. Leave to set.

7 With a small palette knife, spread the tempered chocolate thinly onto the acetate, completely covering the whole sheet and the gold cocoa butter. When almost set, remove the layer of tape securing it to the tray and roll the sheet up gently (chocolate on the inside) forming a tube. Secure with tape and seal the inside seam with more tempered chocolate. Repeat with the remaining acetate sheets. Leave to set for 30 minutes in a cool, dry area.

Meanwhile, make the espresso syrup:

8 Prepare the espresso coffee, mix in the sugar until dissolved and leave to cool. Add the rum and store in an airtight container until needed.

Next, make the mascarpone mousse:

9 Put the egg yolks, sugar and vanilla seeds into a mixing bowl over a gentle bain-marie (water bath). Whisk the mixture continuously for about 10 minutes until light and fluffy. Take off the heat, whisking occasionally until cool.

10 Put the cream in a mixing bowl and whisk until it forms soft peaks. In a separate bowl, beat the mascarpone until smooth.

11 Take one-third of the sabayon and mix it into the mascarpone. Mix until it is smooth, then fold in the rest of the sabayon. Lastly fold in the whipped cream and use immediately.

To assemble & finish:

12 Dip 12 biscuits à la cuillère in the espresso syrup and top each one with a disc of chocolate jelly. Place a chocolate casket on top of each one so that they form the base of the dessert.

13 Spoon the mascarpone mousse into a piping (pastry) bag fitted with a 12mm (½ inch) fluted nozzle (tip). Pipe mousse into each casket until they are half full. Dip the remaining biscuits in espresso syrup, place another jelly disc on top and then carefully add one to each casket. Fill the caskets with more mascarpone mousse, piping so that you finish with a swirl on top.

14 Gently dust the top of each casket with cocoa powder and sprinkle with chopped cocoa nibs. Leave to set for at least 2 hours in the fridge.

15 When you are ready to serve, use a sharp knife or scalpel to cut the tape holding the acetate onto the caskets and gently peel it off. Decorate each casket with a chocolate copeaux.

DARK CHOCOLATE & SESAME PARFAIT
sandwiched with chocolate galettes

Parfait, meaning 'perfect' in French, is literally that — lighter and more delicate than ice cream due to the sabayon being much more aerated.

Makes 12

For the parfait
125g (4½oz) fine dark (bittersweet) chocolate (63% cocoa solids), finely chopped
180ml (6fl oz/¾ cup) whipping (pouring) cream (30% butter fat)
120g (4¼oz) egg yolks (about 6 eggs)
70g (2½oz/⅓ cup) caster (superfine) sugar
25g (scant 1oz) ready-made white sesame paste (see page 224)
12g (⅓ oz) ready-made dark sesame paste (see page 224)

For the chocolate galettes
1 quantity Chocolate Biscuit Dough (see Hollandaise Biscuits, page 148)
Egg wash (see page 144)

Flavour Variation

To make **White Chocolate & Sudatchi (Japanese lime) Parfait**, follow the dark (bittersweet) chocolate parfait recipe above, but replace the dark (bittersweet) chocolate with 160g (5½oz) fine white chocolate (heat over a bain-marie/water bath to 40°C/104°F) and replace the sesame pastes with 3g (½ tsp) grated sudatchi or lime zest.

To make Vanilla Galettes, use the Vanilla Biscuit Dough on page 148 and continue as with the Chocolate Galettes above.

To make the chocolate galettes:

1 Preheat the oven to 180°C (350°F/ Gas 4). Roll the chocolate sablé dough out to 4mm (⅛ inch) depth on a lightly floured work surface and use a 5cm (2 inch) fluted cutter to cut 24 rounds from the dough. Transfer the rounds to a baking tray (sheet) lined with a non-stick baking mat and leave to rest for1 hour in the fridge.

2 Brush with egg wash and bake in the preheated oven for 10–12 minutes. Leave to cool.

To make the parfait:

3 Line a baking tray (sheet) with silicone (baking) paper and place twelve 5cm (2 inch) metal rings with a depth of 2cm (¾ inch) on top (make in batches if you don't have enough metal rings). Transfer to the freezer until needed.

4 Melt the chocolate over a bain-marie (water bath) until it reaches 45°C (113°F). Put the cream into a mixing bowl and whisk until soft peaks form, about 5 minutes. Alternatively, whisk in an electric mixer fitted with the whisk attachment.

5 Put the egg yolks and sugar into a separate mixing bowl over a gently heated bain-marie (water bath) and begin to gradually whisk until the mixture is very light and holding its shape. The sabayon is now cooked and should be the consistency of semi-melted ice cream. Take off the heat and continue to whisk over a bowl of ice water until cool (this prevents the mixture from splitting).

6 Mix both of the sesame pastes into the melted chocolate. Mix the sabayon into the whipped cream and then gradually fold in the melted chocolate mixture in three stages.

7 Spoon the mixture into a piping (pastry) bag, snip a hole in the end and pipe into the metal rings on the prepared baking tray (sheet). Freeze overnight.

8 When you are ready to serve, remove the metal rings from the parfait and sandwich each parfait circle between two chocolate galettes, leave to soften slightly for 5 minutes before serving.

CHOCOLATE & PEANUT ICE CREAM

Quality ice cream seems to be getting more and more popular, and to reflect this we built a specialized cabinet in our Belgravia store, where this ice cream is one of the most popular.

Serves 10–12

500ml (16fl oz/2 cups) whole milk
150ml (5fl oz/⅔ cup) double (heavy) cream
100g (3½oz) egg yolks (about 5 eggs)
85g (3oz/generous ⅓ cup) caster (superfine) sugar
50g (1¾oz/½ cup) cocoa powder
75g (2½oz) fine dark (bittersweet) chocolate (63% cocoa solids), chopped
175g (6oz) **Praline Paste** *(see pages 158–159)*, made with 200g (7oz) unsalted roasted peanuts and 100g (3½oz) salted roasted peanuts

1 Put the milk and cream in a saucepan and bring to the boil.

2 Meanwhile, whisk the egg yolks and sugar together in a mixing bowl until light in colour, about 2–3 minutes. Add the cocoa powder and mix until smooth.

> **Note:** You will need an ice cream machine.

3 Pour half of the boiled milk and cream over the egg yolk mixture and whisk until fully mixed. Transfer the egg yolk mixture back to the milk and cream in the saucepan.

4 Cook over a gentle heat, stirring continuously, until the mixture reaches 82–84°C (179–183°F) – the custard should be thick enough to coat the back of a spoon. Take off the heat and pass through a fine sieve (strainer) into a bowl containing the chopped chocolate. Mix until the chocolate has melted and is completely smooth. Cool rapidly, ideally over an ice bain-marie (water bath).

5 Add 85g (3oz) of the praline paste to the custard and mix through. Pour into a plastic container, cover and leave overnight in the fridge to allow the custard to develop and improve in flavour *(see Tip below)*.

6 Churn the mixture in an ice cream machine following the manufacturer's instructions. Once churned, fold through the remaining praline paste.

Tip: Leaving the custard overnight before churning is an ideal scenario as it will help the flavours meld together. However, if you do not have enough time for this you can churn the custard as soon as it has cooled.

CHOCOLATE & RASPBERRY SORBET

A sorbet gives you a cleaner and more intense chocolate flavour and the raspberry purée brings out its fruity characteristics. The lace tuille this is finished with creates an eye-catching dish.

Serves 8–10

250ml (9fl oz/1 cup) water
130g (4½oz/generous ½ cup) caster (superfine) sugar
75g (2½oz/¾ cup) cocoa powder
150g (5½oz) fine dark (bittersweet) chocolate (63% cocoa solids), roughly chopped
300g (10oz) raspberry purée (see Blackcurrant Purée, page 124)

For the chocolate lace tuile (makes about 10 tuiles)
40g (1½oz/¼ cup) plain (all-purpose) flour
7g (1 tsp) cocoa powder
60ml (2fl oz/¼ cup) milk
150g (5½oz/⅔ cup) jam or preserving sugar
50g (1¾oz/4 tbsp) unsalted butter

Note: You will need an ice cream machine.

To make the chocolate lace tuile:

1 Preheat the oven to 180°C (350°F/ Gas 4). Sift the flour and cocoa powder into a mixing bowl.

2 Put the milk, sugar and butter into a small saucepan and bring to the boil, then cook over a low heat for 2 minutes, stirring continuously. Take off the heat, add the dry ingredients and mix until smooth.

3 Spread half of the mixture thinly onto a non-stick baking mat using an angled palette knife and place a sheet of silicone (baking) paper on top. Cook in the preheated oven for 4–5 minutes until the mixture has spread and holes or a lattice pattern have

appeared. Leave to cool and repeat with the remaining mixture. Carefully pull away from the silicone (baking) paper, break into shards and store in an airtight container until needed.

To make the sorbet:

4 Put the water and sugar in a saucepan and bring to the boil. Add the cocoa powder and continue to cook over a low heat for 2–3 minutes.

5 Pass the mixture through a fine sieve (strainer) into a bowl containing the chopped chocolate. Mix until the chocolate has melted and it is completely smooth. Cool rapidly over an ice bain-marie (water bath) and then mix in the raspberry purée.

6 Churn the mixture in an ice cream machine following the manufacturer's instructions. Serve the sorbet with the chocolate lace tuiles.

ORANGE & YOGURT ICE CREAM LOLLIES dipped in chocolate & cocoa nibs
This recipe dates back to my time with Anton Edelmann at The Savoy, where it was always a favourite.

Makes 8–10 large lollies/40 petit fours

For the orange & yogurt ice cream
500ml (16fl oz/2 cups) orange juice
185g (6½oz/generous ¾ cup) caster
   (superfine) sugar
120g (4¼oz) egg yolks (about 6 eggs)
225g (7oz) crème fraîche
275g (10oz) natural Greek yogurt
Grated zest of 2 oranges

For the dipping & decoration
300g (10oz) fine dark (bittersweet)
   chocolate (63% cocoa solids), chopped
150g (5½oz) cocoa butter, chopped
35g (generous 1oz) cocoa nibs

Note: You will need an ice cream machine and lolly moulds and sticks.

1 Put the orange juice in a pan and boil and reduce for about 10 minutes to 300ml (½ pint). Once reduced, add 85g (3oz) of the sugar. Meanwhile, whisk the egg yolks with the remaining sugar in a bowl until light in colour. Pour half of the reduced juice over the egg yolk mixture and whisk until mixed. Transfer back to the orange juice in the saucepan and cook over a gentle heat, stirring continuously, until it reaches 82–84°C (179–183°F) and is thick enough to coat the back of a spoon. Take off the heat and pass through a fine sieve (strainer). Cool rapidly over an ice bain-marie (water bath).

2 Once cool, whisk in the crème fraîche, yogurt and zest until fully combined. Pour into a container and chill overnight to allow the custard to improve in flavour (see Tip, page 202). Churn in an ice cream machine following the manufacturer's instructions.

3 Spoon the churned ice cream into the lolly moulds. Freeze for about 1 hour. Take out of the freezer and place a lolly stick into the centre of each mould. Return to the freezer overnight. To make the dipping chocolate, melt the chocolate and cocoa butter over a bain-marie (water bath) to 45°C (113°F), then leave to cool to 38°C (100°F). Demould the lollies, dip them in the chocolate and sprinkle with the cocoa nibs. Return to the freezer again to fully set.

ALMOND MILK ICE CREAM LOLLIES dipped in nutty chocolate
I love crunching through the dark (bittersweet) chocolate coating to reveal the creamy, almond ice cream.

Makes 8–10 large lollies/40 petit fours

For the almond milk ice cream
500ml (16fl oz/2 cups) milk
60g (2oz/generous ¼ cup)
   lightly roasted almonds
200ml (7fl oz/generous ¾ cup)
   double (heavy) cream
125g (4½oz/generous ½ cup)
   caster (superfine) sugar
120g (4oz) egg yolks (about 6 eggs)

For the dipping & decoration
300g (10oz) fine dark (bittersweet)
   chocolate (63% cocoa solids), chopped
150g (5½oz) cocoa butter, chopped
35g (generous 1oz) roasted almonds,
   finely chopped

Note: You will need an ice cream machine and lolly moulds and sticks.

1 Put the milk in a saucepan and bring to a light boil. Add the almonds and cook over a low heat for 5 minutes. Transfer to a food processor or blender and blitz to a paste. Pass the mixture through a fine sieve (strainer) and transfer it to a clean saucepan. Add the cream and 100g (3½oz/ scant ½ cup) of the sugar and bring to the boil.

2 Meanwhile, whisk the egg yolks and the remaining sugar together in a mixing bowl until light in colour, about 2–3 minutes. Pour half of the boiled milk over the egg yolk mixture and whisk until fully mixed. Transfer this mixture back to the milk in the saucepan and cook over a gentle heat, stirring continuously, until it reaches 82–84°C (179–183°F) – the mixture should be thick enough to coat the back of a spoon. Take off the heat and pass through a fine sieve (strainer). Cool rapidly, ideally over an ice bain-marie (water bath). Pour into a container and chill overnight to allow the custard to improve in flavour (see Tip, page 202). Churn the mixture in an ice cream machine following the manufacturer's instructions.

3 Spoon the churned ice cream into the lolly moulds. Freeze for about 1 hour. Take out of the freezer and place a lolly stick into the centre of each mould. Return to the freezer overnight. To make the dipping chocolate, melt the chocolate and cocoa butter over a bain-marie (water bath) to 45°C (113°F), then leave to cool to 38°C (100°F). Demould the lollies, dip them into the chocolate and sprinkle with the chopped almonds. Return to the freezer again to fully set.

CHOCOLATE & COFFEE ICE CREAM in a chocolate cone

Making your own cones may seem like a lot of effort, but it's definitely worth it and the end results are always impressive.

Makes about 12–15

For the chocolate cones
150ml (5fl oz/⅔ cup) orange juice
200g (7oz/scant 1 cup) jam
  or preserving sugar
100g (3½oz/1 stick) unsalted butter
40g (1½oz/3 tbsp) liquid glucose
65g (2¼oz/scant ½ cup) plain
  (all-purpose) flour, sifted
10g (¼oz) cocoa powder, sifted
70g (2½oz) desiccated coconut
30g (1oz) hazelnuts, finely chopped

For the chocolate & coffee ice cream
500ml (16fl oz/2 cups) milk
4g (½ tsp) ground espresso coffee
120ml (4fl oz/½ cup) double
  (heavy) cream
120g (4¼oz) egg yolk (about 6 eggs)
85g (3oz/generous ⅓ cup) caster
  (superfine) sugar
50g (1¾oz/½ cup) cocoa powder
75g (2½oz) fine dark (bittersweet)
  chocolate (63% cocoa solids), chopped
Cocoa nibs, roughly chopped, to decorate

Make the chocolate cones in advance:

1 Preheat the oven to 180°C (350°F/ Gas 4). Put the orange juice, sugar, butter and glucose in a saucepan and bring to the boil. Mix in the flour and cocoa powder. Stirring continuously, continue to cook over a low heat for 2–3 minutes. Take off the heat and mix in the coconut and hazelnuts. Leave to cool.

2 Draw 20cm (8 inch) diameter semi-circle stencils onto an upside-down piece of silicone (baking) paper placed on a non-stick baking mat. Use a palette knife to spread about 25g (scant 1oz) of the mixture into each stencil. You will need 15 in total (you will have to cook in batches). Cook in

the oven for 4–5 minutes until lace-like and coloured. Remove from the oven, leave to cool slightly and then shape each semi-circle around a cone mould (pastry horn moulds are ideal, *see page 224*) overlapping the edges to seal. Leave to cool completely then store in an airtight container until needed.

To make the ice cream:

3 Put the milk and coffee in a pan and bring to the boil. Take off the heat, cover with cling film (plastic wrap) and leave to infuse for 20 minutes. Pass through a fine sieve (strainer) and return to a clean pan. Add the cream and bring to the boil. Meanwhile, whisk the egg yolks and sugar together in a mixing bowl until light in colour, about 2–3 minutes. Stir in the cocoa powder and mix until smooth.

4 Pour half of the boiled milk over the egg yolk mixture and whisk until fully mixed. Transfer back to the milk in the saucepan and cook over a gentle heat, stirring continuously, until it reaches 82–84°C (179–183°F). Take off the heat and pass through a fine sieve (strainer) into a bowl containing the chopped chocolate. Stir until the chocolate has completely melted and smooth. Cool rapidly, ideally over an ice bain-marie (water bath).

5 Pour the mixture into a plastic container, cover and leave overnight in the fridge to allow the custard to develop and improve in flavour *(see Tip, page 202)*. Churn in an ice cream machine following the manufacturer's instructions. Spoon the churned ice cream into a piping (pastry) bag fitted with an 8mm (⅓ inch) fluted nozzle (tip) and pipe the ice cream into the cones. Serve immediately.

Flavour Variations

Gianduja Ice Cream in a chocolate cone:
To make the ice cream, follow the chocolate & coffee ice cream recipe but omit the espresso coffee in the first step and replace the cocoa powder and dark (bittersweet) chocolate with 225g (8oz) gianduja and 25g (scant 1oz) Praline Paste *(see pages 158–159)*. Serve in chocolate cones as opposite.

Caramelized White Chocolate & Miso Ice Cream in a coconut & orange cone:
To make the ice cream, first caramelize 240g (8½oz) roughly chopped fine white chocolate by baking it on a baking tray (sheet) lined with a non-stick baking mat in an oven preheated to 130°C (250°F/Gas ½) for 90 minutes until lightly golden (stir and spread the chocolate every 20 minutes with a palette knife to ensure the caramelization is even). Now follow the chocolate & coffee ice cream recipe, replacing the coffee with 50g (1¾oz) miso paste, the dark (bittersweet) chocolate with the caramelized white chocolate and omit the cocoa powder. To make the cones, follow the chocolate cone recipe, but replace the cocoa powder, desiccated coconut and chopped hazelnuts with 100g (3½oz) desiccated coconut.

> **Note:** You will need an ice cream machine.

Opposite from left to right: Gianduja Ice Cream in a chocolate cone; Chocolate & Coffee Ice Cream in a chocolate cone; and Caramelized White Chocolate & Miso Ice Cream in a coconut & orange cone.

DARK CHOCOLATE GRANITA
with poached brambles
In our dessert bar we serve this as a pre-dessert. It's lovely and refreshing and great for cleansing the palate.

Serves 10–12

500ml (16fl oz/2 cups) water
100g (3½oz/scant ½ cup) caster (superfine) sugar
½ vanilla pod (bean), split lengthways
35g (1¼oz/generous ¼ cup) cocoa powder, sifted
60g (2oz) fine dark (bittersweet) chocolate (63% cocoa solids), chopped

For the brambles

200ml (7fl oz/generous ¾ cup) water
200g (7oz/scant 1 cup) caster (superfine) sugar
½ vanilla pod (bean), split lengthways
250g (9oz) brambles (or blackberries)

Flavour Variation

To make **Milk Chocolate & Jasmine Granita with Poached Apricots**, follow the recipe for Dark Chocolate Granita above, but replace the cocoa powder with 10g (¼oz) jasmine tea leaves and leave to infuse for 2–3 hours. Re-boil and strain over 60g (2oz) finely chopped fine milk chocolate, mix until smooth, then continue with the recipe from step 4. To make the poached apricots, make the bramble recipe above using 100g (3½oz) caster (superfine) sugar and replacing the brambles with 600g (1¼lb) stoned and quartered apricots. Let them cook for 3–4 minutes before taking off the heat.

To make the poached brambles:

1. Put the water and sugar in a saucepan. Scrape the seeds from the split vanilla pod (bean) into the saucepan and drop in the empty pod, too. Bring to the boil and then add the brambles. Take off the heat and leave to cool (the residual heat will cook the brambles).

To make the granita:

2. Put the serving dishes in the freezer for at least 30 minutes. Put the water and sugar in a saucepan. Scrape the seeds from the split vanilla pod (bean) into the saucepan and drop in the empty pod, too. Bring to the boil.

3. Add the cocoa powder, whisk together and cook over a low heat for 2–3 minutes. Take off the heat and pass the mixture through a fine sieve (strainer) into a mixing bowl containing the chopped chocolate. Mix until smooth.

4. Cool the mixture rapidly, ideally over an ice bain-marie (water bath). Pour into a wide shallow dish (the shallower the container, the quicker the granita will freeze). Freeze for 1–2 hours until it is solid around the edges.

5. Remove the granita from the freezer and scrape the ice with a fork, mixing it from the edges into the centre. Return to the freezer. Repeat this scraping and mixing process every 30 minutes until the entire mixture has turned into small, separated ice flakes; this will take about 2 hours.

6. When ready to serve, rake with a fork to loosen the granita and separate the ice flakes and spoon into the chilled serving dishes. Top with the poached brambles.

VANILLA ICE CREAM & CHOCOLATE SAUCE

This combination is an age-old classic. Warm chocolate sauce over creamy vanilla ice cream – need I say more?

Serves 8–10

For the vanilla ice cream
500ml (16fl oz/2 cups) milk
200ml (7fl oz/generous ¾ cup) double (heavy) cream
125g (4½oz/generous ½ cup) caster (superfine) sugar
1 vanilla pod (bean), split lengthways
120g (4¼oz) egg yolks (about 6 eggs)

For the chocolate sauce
150ml (5½fl oz/⅔ cup) milk
35ml (1fl oz/1 tbsp) double (heavy) cream
30g (1oz) caster (superfine) sugar
200g (7oz) fine dark (bittersweet) chocolate (66% cocoa solids), chopped
30g (1oz/2 tbsp) unsalted butter, cut into cubes and at room temperature

To make the vanilla ice cream:

1 Put the milk, cream and 60g (2oz/¼ cup) of the sugar in a saucepan. Scrape the seeds from the split vanilla pod (bean) into the saucepan and drop in the empty pod, too. Bring to the boil. Meanwhile, whisk the egg yolks and the remaining sugar together in a mixing bowl until light in colour, about 2–3 minutes.

> **Note:** You will need an ice cream machine.

2 Pour half of the boiled milk mixture over the egg yolk mixture and whisk until fully mixed. Transfer the egg yolk mixture back to the milk in the saucepan and cook over a gentle heat, stirring continuously, repeat until it reaches 82–84°C (179–183°F) – the mixture should be thick enough to coat the back of a spoon. Take off the heat and pass through a fine sieve (strainer). Cool rapidly, ideally over an ice bain-marie (water bath).

3 Pour the mixture into a plastic container, cover and leave overnight in the fridge to allow the custard to develop and improve in flavour *(see Tip, page 202).*

4 Churn the mixture in an ice cream machine following the manufacturer's instructions.

Make the chocolate sauce just before you are ready to serve:

5 Put the milk, cream and sugar in a saucepan and bring to the boil. Pour over the chopped chocolate in a mixing bowl and mix until smooth and completely melted. Stir in the butter and mix until fully emulsified.

6 Serve the ice cream in individual chilled serving bowls with the chocolate sauce poured over.

CHOCOLATE & PRALINE SPREAD with brioche

Equally perfect as a lazy weekend breakfast in bed and a contemporary afternoon tea.

Makes 8–10 slices

For the brioche

200g (7oz/1⅓ cups) plain (all-purpose) flour, sifted, plus a little extra for dusting the tin (pan)

30g (1oz) caster (superfine) sugar

6g (1 tsp) salt

10g (¼oz) fresh yeast

140g (5oz) whole eggs (about 3 eggs)

120g (4¼oz) unsalted butter, cut into cubes and at room temperature, plus a little extra for greasing the tin (pan)

Egg wash (see page 144)

For the chocolate & praline spread

200ml (7fl oz/generous ¾ cup) whipping (pouring) cream

175g (6oz) fine milk chocolate (35% cocoa solids), finely chopped

50g (1¾oz) fine dark (bittersweet) chocolate (66% cocoa solids), finely chopped

175g (6oz) Praline Paste (see pages 158–159)

> **Note:** You will need one 18 × 8 × 7.5cm (7 × 3¼ × 3 inch) loaf tin (pan).

To make the brioche:

1 Put the flour, sugar and salt into the bowl of an electric mixer fitted with the dough hook. In a separate bowl, crumble the yeast into the eggs and mix. Add this to the dry ingredients.

2 Mix on a moderate speed for 10–12 minutes until the mixture becomes elastic and comes away from the side of the bowl. Gradually add in the butter and continue to mix until the mixture comes away from the side of the bowl again.

3 Cover the bowl with cling film (plastic wrap) and leave to rest and prove until it doubles in size, about 30 minutes. Knock back the dough and transfer to the fridge for at least 1 hour. Preheat the oven to 200°C (400°F/Gas 6) and lightly grease and dust the tin (pan) with flour.

4 Place the dough into the tin (pan). Leave to prove until doubled in size. Brush the top of the loaf with egg wash and bake in the preheated oven for 25–30 minutes until golden in colour. Reduce the oven temperature to 180°C (350°F/Gas 4) and cook for another

6–8 minutes. Leave to cool in the tin for a few minutes and then turn out onto a wire rack to cool completely.

To make the spread:

5 Put the cream in a saucepan, bring to the boil and then pour over the chopped chocolate in a mixing bowl and mix until smooth. Stir in the praline paste, mix again and then pour into a sterilized jar and leave to cool. (The spread will keep for 1 week stored in a cool, dark area.) Serve the brioche cut into slices with the chocolate spread.

WHITE CHOCOLATE MATCHA LATTE
& Green Tea Cakes

I predict matcha lattes will be the next big thing – they are very popular in Japan. We add white chocolate, which complements the matcha.

**Makes 2 lattes,
plus 32 small oval tea cakes**

For the green tea cakes
125g (4½oz/1¼ sticks) unsalted butter,
   cut into cubes
115g (4oz) egg whites (about 4 eggs)
125g (4½oz/generous ½ cup) caster
   (superfine) sugar
115g (4oz/1½ cups) ground almonds
15g (½oz/1 tbsp) ground hazelnuts
5g (1 tsp) matcha (green tea powder)
40g (1½oz) plain (all-purpose) flour,
   sifted
Black & white toasted sesame seeds,
   to sprinkle

For the white chocolate matcha latte
5g (½ tsp) matcha powder
10ml (¾ tbsp) water
500ml (16fl oz/2 cups) whole milk
80g (2¾oz) fine white chocolate,
   finely chopped

> **Note:** You will need two
> 16-oval hole silicone moulds.

To make the green tea cakes:

1 Make a beurre noisette. Put the butter in a saucepan and heat until the butter becomes golden and has a nutty aroma. Leave to cool.

2 Beat the egg whites and sugar together by hand in a mixing bowl and add the ground almonds, hazelnuts and matcha powder. Stir in the beurre noisette.

3 Mix in the sifted flour and continue to mix by hand. Transfer to the fridge to rest for at least 30 minutes. Preheat the oven to 160°C (325°F/Gas 3).

4 Transfer the dough mixture to a piping bag fitted with a 15mm (¾ inch) plain piping nozzle (tip) and pipe the mixture into the moulds, leaving a small gap below the rim of each mould. Sprinkle the tops of each cake with the white and black sesame seeds. Bake in the preheated oven for about 20 minutes until golden brown and the cakes spring back when pressed. Leave to cool before removing the cakes from the mould. Store in an airtight container.

To make the latte:

5 Mix the matcha powder and water in a small bowl to make a paste (use a Japanese or normal whisk to eliminate any lumps).

6 Place the milk and the matcha paste in a saucepan over a moderate heat and whisk continuously until the mixture simmers. Take off the heat and pour over the chopped white chocolate in a bowl. Stir until fully emulsified, then use an Aerolatte whisk to make it very light and foamy.

7 Fill 2 serving cups two-thirds of the way with the matcha milk and spoon the froth onto the top, filling each cup. Serve with the green tea cakes.

BLACK FOREST MILKSHAKE

This is an adult milkshake – I love the idea of taking the classic flavours of black forest and making them into a drink.

Makes 2

150g (5½oz) **Chocolate Ice Cream** *(see page 206)*, omitting the coffee
85g (3oz) **Vanilla Ice Cream** *(see page 210)*
200ml (7fl oz/generous ¾ cup) whole milk
100g (3½oz) **Cherry Compote** *(see page 177)*
Griottine cherries *(see Glossary, page 224)*, to decorate
½ fine dark chocolate block, for shavings to decorate *(see page 106)*

1 Put all of the ingredients (except the griottine cherries) in a stainless steel container or measuring jug and blitz with a hand-held blender.

2 Pour into tall glasses, decorate with griottine cherries and chocolate shavings and serve immediately.

CHILLED MINT CHOCOLATE DRINK
with crème chantilly

Chocolate and mint is a classic combination, and this cool drink with sweet chantilly is refreshing yet indulgent.

Makes 4

500ml (16fl oz/2 cups) whole milk
7g (⅓oz) fresh mint leaves
75g (2½oz) fine dark (bittersweet) chocolate (with 70% cocoa solids), roughly chopped
1 quantity **Crème Chantilly** *(see page 162)*
Chocolate copeaux *(see page 153)* and mint sprigs, to decorate

1 Put the milk in a saucepan and bring to the boil. Take off the heat and add the mint leaves to the pan. Cover with cling film (plastic wrap) and leave to infuse for 30 minutes.

2 Pass the milk through a fine sieve (strainer) to remove and discard the mint leaves and return the milk to the saucepan. Bring to the boil again and then pour this over the chopped chocolate in a mixing bowl or jug. Mix until smooth. Cool rapidly, ideally over an ice bain-marie (water bath).

3 Fill 4 serving glasses three-quarters full with the chilled chocolate and mint drink. Warm a teaspoon and make a quenelle of crème chantillly. Place a quenelle on top of each drink and decorate with chocolate shavings and a sprig of mint.

CHOCOLATE MILKSHAKE

Chocolate milkshakes remind me of childhood memories. I use dark (bittersweet) chocolate ice cream so it is gloriously decadent.

Makes 2

280ml (9½fl oz/generous 1 cup) whole milk
300g (10oz) **Chocolate Ice Cream** *(see page 206)*, omitting the coffee

1 Put all of the ingredients in a stainless steel container or measuring jug and blitz with a hand-held blender or whisk together by hand in a bowl (the ice cream would have to be fairly soft to be able to whisk by hand).

2 Pour into tall glasses and serve immediately.

Opposite from left to right: Black Forest Milkshake; Chilled Milk Chocolate Drink; Chocolate Milkshake.

TROPICAL BREEZE
A perfect cocktail for dinner parties.

WHITE CHOCOLATE MARTINI
A chocolate twist is given to this classic cocktail.

Makes 4

For the tropical fruit layer
100g (3½ oz) mango purée
  (see Blackcurrant Purée, page 124)
100g (3½oz) passion fruit purée
  (see Blackcurrant Purée, page 124)
25g (scant 1oz) jam or preserving sugar

For the chocolate & rum layer
85g (3oz) fine dark (bittersweet)
  chocolate (70% cocoa solids), chopped
175ml (6fl oz/generous ⅔ cup) water
50g (1¾oz/¼ cup) caster
  (superfine) sugar
75ml (2½fl oz/scant ⅓ cup) dark rum

For the coconut foam
100g (3½oz) ready-made coconut purée
  or coconut milk
75ml (2½fl oz/scant ⅓ cup) whipping
  (pouring) cream
30ml (1fl oz) whole milk
25ml (scant 1fl oz/1½ tbsp) Malibu

1 To make the tropical fruit layer, put
the fruit purées together in a saucepan
and bring to the boil. Add the sugar
and cook over a moderate heat for
1–2 minutes. Leave to cool.

2 To make the chocolate layer, place
the chocolate in a large mixing bowl,
put the water and sugar in a saucepan
and bring to the boil. Pour the sugar
syrup over the chocolate and mix until
smooth. Leave to cool and then add
the dark rum.

3 To make the coconut foam, whisk
all the ingredients together in a mixing
bowl to form a light foam.

4 To assemble, spoon the tropical
layer into 4 cocktail glasses. Pour the
chocolate layer on top down the back
of a spoon. Top with the coconut foam.
Stir it just before you drink.

Makes 4 cocktails

Tempered fine dark (bittersweet)
  chocolate (see pages 18–19), for piping
240ml (8fl oz/scant 1 cup) whipping
  (pouring) cream
150g (5½oz) fine white chocolate,
  finely chopped
85g (3oz/generous ⅓ cup) caster
  (superfine) sugar
85ml (3fl oz/⅓ cup) water
100ml (3½fl oz/generous ⅓ cup) vodka
50ml (1¾fl oz/3 tbsp) vermouth

1 Spoon the tempered dark
(bittersweet) chocolate into a
paper piping (pastry) bag and pipe
lines of chocolate into 4 Martini
glasses. Transfer the glasses to the
fridge to chill while you make
the cocktail.

2 Put the cream in a saucepan and
bring to the boil. Pour the cream over
the chopped chocolate in a mixing
bowl or jug and stir until smooth and
emulsified. Leave to cool. Meanwhile,
put the sugar and water in a pan and
bring to the boil. Leave to cool.

3 Pour the vodka, vermouth and
the cooled sugar syrup into a cocktail
shaker and add in the white chocolate
mixture and some ice. Shake until fully
mixed. Pour into the chilled martini
glasses and serve immediately.

INGREDIENTS & EQUIPMENT

INGREDIENTS
Choose your ingredients with care and be prepared to shop around until you find what you are after.

Alcohol You don't need to buy the most expensive brands, but it should be drinkable and something you would enjoy yourself. As you will see dark rum, kirsch and Grand Marnier feature commonly in the Patisserie chapter (see pages 150–197).

Almond Paste (Marzipan) Made up of approximately equal parts of ground blanched almonds and sugar mixed into a paste.

Butter Always use good-quality butter and never substitute with margarine as it has a huge bearing on the quality of your final dish. You will see in the recipes it is important to think ahead at times – for ganache the butter needs to be around 38°C (100°F) to ensure it emulsifies correctly and for cakes it is important to use butter at room temperature.

Coffee & Tea Always buy in locally where possible and spend a little extra for quality – it's worth it.

Cream I tend to only use whipping (pouring) cream for our chocolates and patisserie, although there is the odd exception. I find that double (heavy) cream is too heavy for most recipes. Keep the cream chilled right up until you are ready to use it.

Stages of whipping egg whites

Ribbon Stage – as you lift the whisk from the mixture it will fall back upon itself and a trail or 'ribbon' will be left across the surface. The ribbon will hold shape for a moment, then sink back into the mix.

Soft Peak – when you turn the whisk upside down, the peaks should just be starting to hold. The mix has a soft texture and the peaks will fall back into the mixture after a second.

Stiff Peak – when the whisk is held upside down, the peaks should point straight up without collapsing. The mix is thick and heavy in texture.

Over-beating – after the stiff peak stage, egg whites will start to look grainy and dull. When over beaten, the whisked egg whites will eventually collapse back on themselves.

Eggs All of my recipes are based on large eggs. For consistency I always weigh the eggs (whites and yolks separately) to be sure of the measurement – generally 1 egg yolk is 20g (¾oz), 1 egg white is 30g (1oz) and 1 whole egg is 50g (1¾oz).

Feuillantine Wafers Dried crêpes, wonderful for texture in Patisserie and Bouchées.

Fine Chocolate (couverture) For a number of years Suzue and I have been proud ambassadors for Amedei. They work directly with the growers of the cocoa they use and are completely involved in every stage of the process. Thus producing some of the finest couverture chocolate available (Chuao, Toscano 70 and 63, Toscano Milk and Gianduja to name a few).

Flour Virtually all of my recipes are based on T55, a medium-strength French flour. If this is difficult to get hold of I would suggest sticking with a good-quality plain (all-purpose) flour.

Fresh Herbs Grow your own where possible and if not, buy from a local supplier or market, where they will have a more intense flavour and character. Avoid supermarket herbs as they are grown quickly and lack flavour.

Gelatine All of our recipes that include gelatine are based on leaf gelatine, which is available in good food stores. I always weigh it as the weight changes in different brands. You will have to soak the gelatine in cold water, the colder the better, to soften it and then always squeeze out the excess water and dissolve in the appropriate hot mixture as instructed. For powder gelatine follow the manufacturers' instructions.

Gianduja This is made from chocolate, nuts and sugar, normally in equal parts. It takes its name from Gianduja, a Carnival character who represents the archetypal Piedmontese, a native of the Italian region where hazelnut confectionery is common.

Honey Buy at a farmers market or speciality stores. All varieties of honey have their own special characteristics, whether it be lavender or chestnut. My favourite is Richmond Park Honey with its unique clover notes.

Kinako Also known as soya bean flour, it is made by finely grinding roasted soya beans into a powder. You can buy it in oriental/Japanese shops or online.

Matcha This is ground green tea leaves, which you can buy in oriental/Japanese shops and also online. There are many grades and I would suggest spending some time to find your favourite.

Milk Always use whole milk, there is no point in substituting with a low-fat alternative, trust me…

Neige Décor This is icing sugar that does not dissolve in humid conditions.

Nuts Buy them fresh as they don't improve with age – if you don't use them straight away you can always freeze them. They are not always easy to get hold of but Piedmont hazelnuts and Avola almonds are the best.

Spices If you can, buy them whole and grate (e.g nutmeg) or crush with a rolling pin (e.g cardamom or aniseed) as you need them. Once ground they soon lose their distinct flavour, so buy in small quantities and freeze.

Sugar I generally use caster (superfine) sugar in baking. You can use granulated (white) as an alternative, but I find it coarser. Icing (powdered/pure) sugar is also in a few recipes, and is basically pulverized white sugar – always sieve it before use. We also use brown sugars such as muscovado with its own unique rich, malty flavour. We have recently been introduced to Japanese brown sugar – its light molasses flavour brings a new dimension to some recipes. Invert sugar (see page 23) – you could use soft brown sugar, glucose or honey as a substitute.

Vanilla Pods (Beans) You can buy vanilla extract, but I prefer to use the real thing. It can be expensive to buy the best quality vanilla, however the difference in quality is huge. I tend to buy Tahitian with its delicate flavour or Madagascan with its fruitier notes (bourbon and Mexican are also good).

Yuzu This is a Japanese citrus fruit that we use quite a lot in our Japanese-inspired recipes. You can substitute with lemons or limes.

See page 224 for stockists.

EQUIPMENT

I have been fortunate to cook in kitchens with a wonderful array of equipment. Good-quality equipment doesn't come cheap and where I advise using stainless steel bowls and silicone moulds, it's not always essential. I have also had the misfortune of working in kitchens with little space, wonky ovens and little equipment – the secret is being able to adapt. I would always advise to shop around and look online for the best prices.

Acetate Sheets They will bring a contemporary touch to your chocolates and give a shiny finish – they can be bought either plain or embossed.

Bain-Marie (water bath)/Porringer Pot
There are many ways to melt and temper your chocolate, from a simple saucepan with water and a bowl on top to an electric heated bain marie (water bath)… the choice is yours. It does usually come down to cost. To start with I recommend an old fashioned porringer pot, which are great for tempering the chocolate, retaining heat and ideal to dip in. They also prevent any steam from escaping and getting into your chocolate, thus making it thicker.

Baking Trays (Sheets) I prefer rimless baking trays (sheets) and avoid flimsy trays, that will buckle while baking. Recommended size is 25.5 × 30cm (10 × 12 inch). However, if you cannot get hold of this size, just use as close to this size as possible.

Chocolate Moulds You can buy a wide range of moulds, some simply made out of plastic, this will be enough to get you going (although the moulds won't last long). We use polycarbonate moulds, which if you look after them, will last a long time. It's important to polish moulds (and embossed acetate sheets for decorating chocolates) with either cotton wool or any clean t-shirt material in order to get a shiny finish.

Cooling Rack A standard wire rack is useful for cooling cakes and sponges.

Food Processor I use a Thermomix in my kitchen, not the cheapest bit of kit, but very powerful and versatile, and ideal for Praline Paste (see pages 158–159). Good cookshops will have a wide selection; my advice is to buy something sturdy. I also like to use hand blenders in my kitchen: they are easy to use and clean.

Ice-Cream Machine In our business we use a Paco Jet to churn our ice-cream – it uses a revolutionary method of freezing the custard in a canister and churning once frozen, rather than churning the ice cream as you freeze. A small blade turns at vast spins per second, thus creating the lightest, smoothest ice cream. However, we don't all have a huge amount of money to spend, and thankfully there are several inexpensive machines on the market, so shop around to find a good price; remember that you may need to freeze the churning container in advance.

Knives I would strongly advise using knives made from stainless steel. If you look after them they will last you a lifetime. You will need to buy a good-quality steel to sharpen them. Never put them through the dishwasher as it will damage your blades. You will need an office knife, chopping knife, serrated knife, a small, large and an angled palette knife.

Moulds & Tins It's worth investing in a small selection particularly if you are going to make cakes, bouchées or patisserie. I recommend silicone moulds for the bouchées and small cakes as they are flexible and easy to get out. For the loaf cakes you'll need to buy loaf tins, ideally with a silicone lining, likewise for tartlets.

Non-stick Baking Mats I generally use silicone mats, which are flexible sheets of a non-stick material. They can withstand extreme temperatures, are re-useable and you can buy them in cookshops or online. Silicone (baking) paper works equally well.

Pastry Brush For glazing, buttering moulds and for soaking cakes and sponges. I stopped using soft bristle brushes and now use silicone ones as there is no risk of the odd hair being left on a dish.

Pastry Scraper You'll find these a must in a professional kitchen. They are also not an expensive investment. Great for getting all of the dough cleanly out of a mixing bowl and scraping work surfaces clean.

Rolling Pin While technology has improved much equipment available, I still prefer an old-fashioned French style rolling pin, which is simply a spindle of wood. It may be a good idea to keep a separate one for rolling out almond paste, and another for dough work.

Saucepans Buy thick-bottomed pans, ideally with handles that stay cool. Poor-quality pans warp easily, have hot spots and don't last.

Scales Probably the most important piece of equipment in my kitchen, without it you won't go very far. I would recommend a digital set (a reasonably priced set should do the trick), ideally going up in 1g increments to get the fine detail needed.

Sieve (Strainer) A stainless steel fine-mesh sieve (strainer) is best for pouring through creams and custards. Keep a separate sieve (or ideally a drum sieve) for sieving dry ingredients, such as flour and cocoa powder.

Spatula I use these for anything from mixing ganaches to folding in the sabayon into mousse. Go for the heatproof silicone version, ideally with a slight curve on the blade.

Storage Containers Always buy plastic containers with airtight lids, this will keep your ingredients and mixes fresher for longer.

Tart Moulds & Mousse Frames Buy tartlet moulds that are non-stick and frames that are strong and don't bend, ideally stainless steel.

Thermometer For chocolate work, and particularly for beginners, it would be advisable to invest in an electric thermometer for accuracy. It is also great for custards and pâté de fruit. It's also worth checking your oven temperature periodically with an oven thermometer.

Timers Many ovens have these built in, but ideally buy a digital timer, as time is everything in a baking kitchen – you won't regret it.

Whisk Go for good-quality whisks that can withstand a good beating. I prefer stainless steel whisks. Balloon whisks are excellent for whipping cream or egg whites if you don't have a mixing machine. I would recommend a straight whisk with a long handle for whisking in pans.

See page 224 for stockists.

INDEX

Figures in italics indicate captions.

DIRECTORY

INGREDIENTS

COUVERTURE CHOCOLATE
Amedei
www.kingsfinefood.co.uk
www.amedei-us.com
www.lario.com.au

OTHER COUVERTURE CHOCOLATE
Valrhona – www.chocolate.co.uk
World Wide Chocolate
http://worldwidechocolate.com
Amano Artisan Chocolate
www.amanochocolate.com
Guittard Chocolate Company
www.guittard.com
Michel Cluizel
www.tcfinefoods.co.uk
www.chocosphere.com
Scarffen Berger www.scharffenberger.com
Simon Johnson www.simonjohnson.com
Albert Uster Imports
www.auiswisscatalogue.com/1-CHOC/
Chocolate.html

PATISSERIE & CHOCOLATE INGREDIENTS
London Fine Foods www.efoodies.co.uk
Wild Harvest www.wildharvestuk.com

JAPANESE INGREDIENTS
Keisho Limited www.keisholimited.co.uk
Atari-Ya Foods www.atariya.co.uk
Asian Food Grocer
www.asianfoodgrocer.com

SPICES & SALTS
Speciality Fine Foods
www.specialityfinefoods.org.uk
India Tree www.indiatree.com

FINE TEAS & QUALITY COFFEE
TeaSmith www.teasmith.co.uk
Square Mile Coffee Roasters
http://shop.squaremilecoffee.com/

EQUIPMENT

CHOCOLATE EQUIPMENT AND MOULDS
Deco'Relief www.deco-relief.fr
Home Chocolate Factory
www.homechocolatefactory.com
The Chocolate Mold Factory
www.thechocolatemoldfactory.com
Hilliard's Chocolate System
www.hilliardschocolate.com
Chef Rubber www.chefrubber.com
Chocoley http://chocoley.com
Savour Chocolate & Patisserie School
www.savourschool.com.au
Albert Uster Imports
www.auiswisscatalogue.com/1-CHOC/
Chocolate.html

STENCILS & DECORATIONS
PCB (France) www.pcb-creation.fr
Squires Kitchen www.squires-shop.com
Sugarcraft www.sugarcraft.com

KITCHEN EQUIPMENT
Russums www.russums-shop.co.uk
Amazon www.amazon.co.uk
www.amazon.com
Silicone Moulds.com
www.siliconemoulds.com
Matfer www.matfer.com
Sur la Table www.surlatable.com
Williams-Sonoma
www.williams-sonoma.com
Culinary Cookware
http://www.culinarycookware.com

KITCHENWARE & GLASSES
David Mellor Design
www.davidmellordesign.com

OUR STORES

William Curley
10 Paved Court
Richmond upon Thames TW9 1LZ

William Curley
198 Ebury Street
Belgravia, London SW1W 8UN

William Curley at Harrods
87–135 Brompton Road
Knightsbridge
London SW1X 7XL

www.williamcurley.co.uk

ACKNOWLEDGEMENTS

After years of waiting, I have finally been fortunate enough to find a publisher who shared my vision for this book, so many thanks to Jacqui Small and her hardworking team who have made all this possible. Thanks to Robin Rout for his fabulous design work, to my editor Abi Waters for her endless patience and Jose Lasheras for his expert and stunning photography.

I would like to thank the chefs who gave me such a wonderful training, Pierre Koffmann, Marco Pierre White, Anton Edelmann, Raymond Blanc and Marc Meneau. Not to mention the chefs who took me under their wing when I was an apprentice and to whom I shall always be grateful; Scott Lyall, Willie Pike, Bruce Sangster, Dave Bryson, Benoit Blin, and Ian Ironside who is sadly no longer with us. Also to all the chefs who work so hard for the common good of our beautiful profession.

Special thanks to the team of dedicated young Patissiers and Chocolatiers who have been with our business for a number of years including Mi-Jung Kim, Sarah Frankland, Lucie Bennett, Vicki Stroud, Alistair Birt, Stephanie Almeida, Melissa Paul, Rosie Fickling and Libby Wells.

My gratitude to Alessio and Cecilia Tessieri of Amedei for supplying the best couverture chocolate in the world and to Sir Evelyn Rothschild for his continued patronage. Additionally to Sara Jayne Stanes the chocolate expert, John Kennedy of TeaSmith, The Academy of Chocolate, The Academy of Culinary Arts, Ben Elliott and Christabel McConville of Quintessentially, George Vaughan, and all the team at Tannadice.

Thank you to mine and Suzue's parents and family for their invaluable emotional support.

William Curley